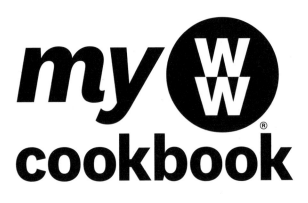

Contents

Welcome

This book will inspire and empower you to cook healthy meals for yourself and those you love. In the following pages, we share super-tasty solutions for breakfast, lunch, and dinner, plus give you the tips to help you throw together great snacks and desserts that you'll turn to time and time again. And of course we've brought you a wealth of delicious recipes that make healthy eating doable in your busy life – many are designed to be on the table in 30 (or even 20!) minutes, while others are ideal for leisurely, celebratory meals, because life has room for both. Here's to a delicious journey – and a happier, healthier you. Enjoy!

Getting started

Lose weight your way

Instead of following someone else's definition of 'healthy', WW gives you the perfect opportunity to discover your own…

WW is the world's top science-based plan for weight loss, but the programme isn't just about the numbers on the scale. Our approach emphasises balance – not only in what you eat. It's a new direction for everyday living, built around enjoyment and the power of healthy habits. Here's how.

You'll eat what you love

Everything's on the menu! The WW programme gives you the freedom to make choices that work. You'll eat well, discover fresh, new flavours and feel good about your new eating habits.

You'll find what moves you

Activity comes naturally when you enjoy what you're doing. Maybe you're already committed to a sport, activity or fitness routine, or perhaps the WW community will help you find a new approach to moving more. Either way, the goal is to feel stronger, more powerful, and proud of what your body can do.

You'll shift your mindset

WW emphasises both thinking in new ways and confronting tough moments with self-compassion. And since WW is a community-based programme, you can turn to your fellow members for support and encouragement in real life and online.

You'll benefit from the power of SmartPoints®

Science-backed and easy to use, the SmartPoints system guides you to a healthier pattern of eating.

Here are some of the basics:
- Every food and drink has a SmartPoints value based on calories, saturated fat, sugar and protein.
- You get a daily SmartPoints Budget to spend on any food or drink you like.
- You'll keep track of your SmartPoints in the WW app.
- Are your weekends different from the rest of your week? Up to 4 daily SmartPoints that you don't use will roll over into your weeklies.

For more flexibility, you have ZeroPoint™ foods

There are many ingredients you don't have to track or measure. Why? It's because they form the foundation of a healthy eating pattern and you have a low risk of overeating them.

How this book can help you every day

1
To help you plan meals more easily, we've divided recipes into chapters on breakfast, lunch, dinner, dessert and snacks. Each chapter begins and ends with either a recipe builder or four easy ways to use common ingredients, to give you a foundation to build upon. Once you're familiar with them, feel free to swap ingredients and experiment.

2
Every recipe includes SmartPoints values for all three WW plans, so it's easy to choose the meals that fit best with your SmartPoints Budget. The 'Recipes by SmartPoints value' index on page 222 lets you see at a glance what will work best for you – you'll even find some recipes that are just 1 or 2 SmartPoints per serving.

3
Need some inspiration? Check out 'Meal planning that works' on page 18. You'll find ideas for cooking ahead, smart shopping and packing great lunches to take to work. We've included a rundown of equipment that makes cooking easy, plus a guide to using spices that proves even the simplest meal can taste sensational.

4
Finally, we've included lots of tips throughout the recipe pages of the book. These will help you get the most out of each recipe, whether they offer advice on how best to make it fit into your eating plan, instructions for how to make it ahead of time, or tips for what to serve it with.

THURSDAY

Courgette, lemon & feta risotto

WEDNESDAY

Banger, baked bean & butternut squash bake

TUESDAY

Tagliatelle tuna puttanesca

SUNDAY

veggie burger

NEXT WEEK

SUNDAY

Turkey shepherds pie

SATURDAY

Peruvian roast chicken with avocado salad

FRIDAY

Feta & black bean nachos

TO BUY
- Feta
- avocado
- capers
- Risotto rice
- Turkey mince

The new basics

With a little time spent planning, cooking healthy meals at home can become second nature. We're here to make it easier and more enjoyable. These answers to common questions should help you on your way.

Quinoa

What makes a meal or a recipe 'healthy'?

The ingredients that go into it play a big part – lots of fresh fruits and veg, lean proteins and healthy fats. Emphasising these foods is the basis for the recipes in this book.

● Most fruits and vegetables are ZeroPoint™ foods on the WW programme, so we include them liberally in recipes.

● Many lean proteins are also either ZeroPoint foods or low in SmartPoints®. WW recommends that you always trim foods of excess fat and remove skin when appropriate.

● Finally, eating proper-size portions is key to weight loss. Our recipes give you exact serving sizes, making it easy for you to track, and they'll highlight what a nutritionally balanced plate should look like.

Are some techniques better for healthy cooking?

Just as all foods are on the menu, WW also embraces all cooking techniques. There are no wrong ways to prep meals and snacks. That said, daily cooking is healthier with techniques that maximise flavour:

● Our recipes often turn to roasting, searing and grilling to develop deep, caramelised flavour naturally, without using a lot of oil.

● Stir-frying can be done with minimal oil, is quick and keeps vegetables colourful and crisp.

● Steaming and poaching are great for locking moisture into foods without using oil or fat.

What swaps make foods tastier and healthier?

Cutting back on added fats, added sugar and added salt can have a big impact on your health in the long run. And in the short run? Cutting back on two out of three of those – fats and sugar – can stretch your SmartPoints Budget. Here are some places to start:

● Swap in healthy, creamy ingredients such as 0% fat natural Greek yogurt, reduced-fat cottage cheese, and buttermilk for all or part of high-fat ingredients such as cream, butter, mayonnaise, and soured cream.

● Reduce the amount of oil you need to keep foods from sticking by using nonstick pans for searing and lining roasting tins with baking paper or kitchen foil.

● Go for fresh and dried herbs and whole and ground spices before you immediately season your food with lots of salt. See 'Smart seasonings' on page 28 for fantastic spice blends that can be used as rubs on lean proteins such as skinless chicken breast fillets.

Easy ways to eat more plants

What can drastically improve both your own health and the health of the planet? Experts agree: eating more plant-based foods. Most of us think of fruits and vegetables when we think of plants, but the category is actually much larger than that. And the WW programme emphasises more plant-based foods than ever.

Oats

Haricot beans

Red lentils

Tofu

Vegan cheese

Grains

Whole grains like brown rice, quinoa, freekeh, barley and oats are fantastic sources of fibre and other nutrients, including many of the same antioxidants found in fruits and vegetables. Go beyond just plonking a spoonful down as a side dish – why not add grains to salads, soups, burger mixes, or your morning breakfast bowl? Try: Smoky bean & barley burgers on page 152.

Beans and lentils

Protein-rich, fibre-packed legumes can be the main event themselves in all sorts of dishes, from soups and stews to tacos. Or, they can boost other ingredients in dishes like chilli, salads, pasta and more. You can keep a few tins around so you always have a stash, or cook up a big pot and freeze the leftovers. Try: Beef & pinto bean chilli on page 134.

Vegan meat and dairy substitutes

Wider interest in plant-based diets means meat and dairy substitutes are now readily available and more varied. Tofu, jackfruit and new varieties of burger patties and sausages that mimic beef, pork and chicken are enticing meat lovers, and a host of non-dairy cheeses and plant-based 'milks' are fun to explore. Try: Jackfruit tacos on page 144.

What's your plan?

When it comes to losing weight and getting healthier, WW knows that what works for one person might not work for someone else. The answer? Three science-backed, proven plans that are tailored to fit your individual needs and personal preferences. Turn to page 16 for an overview on each.

We've developed every recipe in this book to work for all three plans and we've given the SmartPoints® values for each. You can also check out our 'Recipes by SmartPoints value' on page 222, which gives you an instant overview of how different dishes stack up on different plans.

Top tips for smarter tracking

Use these proven tips to make tracking simpler:

1
Pre-track when you can
At the start of each day, think about where you're likely to be and pre-track your food and drinks. This will create a mini meal plan for you and also help you make faster (and better) decisions when you're eating out.

2
Create a backup
It can be hard to remember what you've eaten by the end of the day. That's why it's best to track as you go. But if you find yourself in a bind, put your phone to work. Take a photo of what you're eating so you can track it later in the day.

3
Repeat your successes
Had a successful week of tracking and reaching your goals? Why not use it as a guide to what works for upcoming weeks.

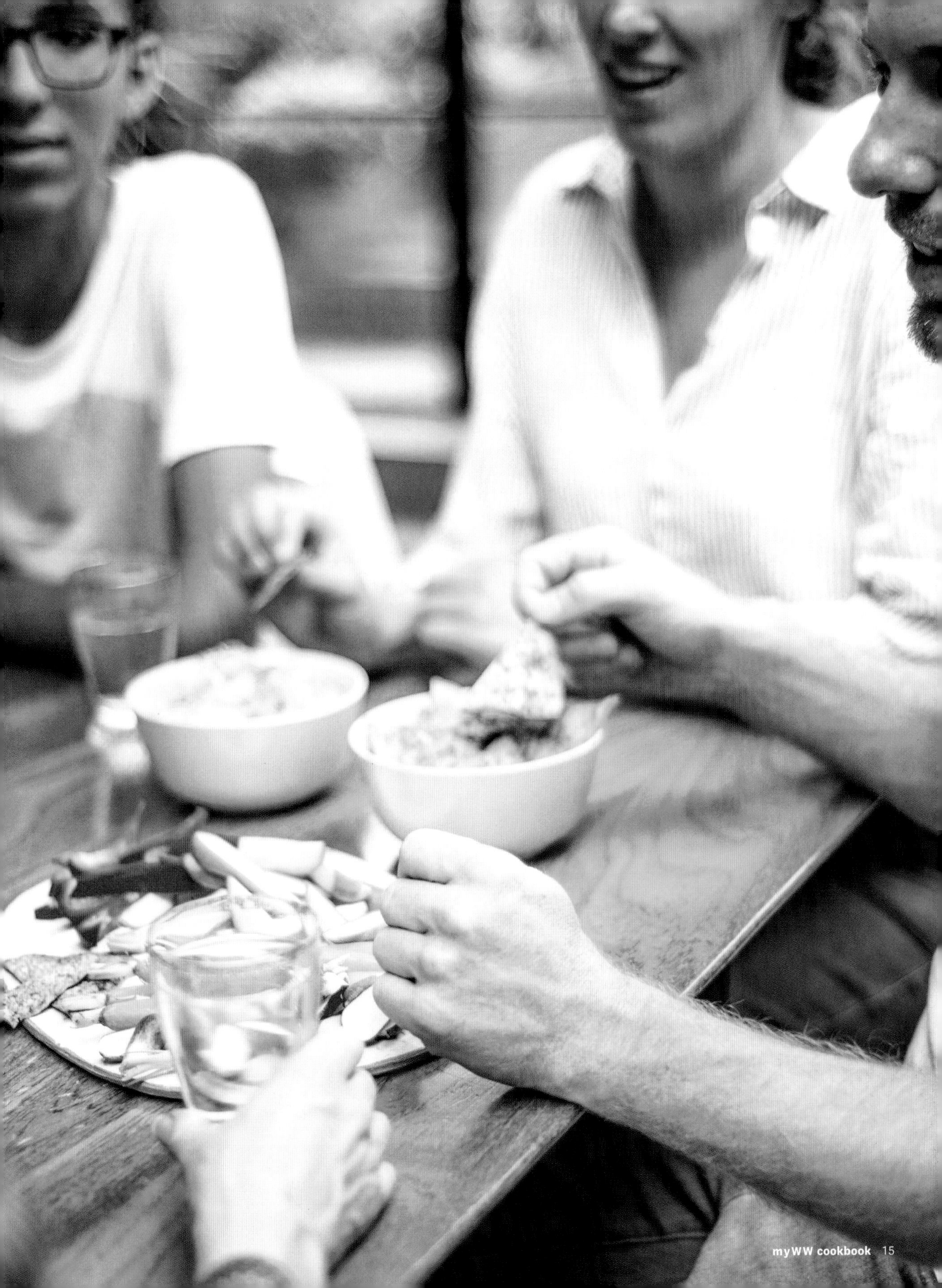

Easy as 1, 2, 3...
Our science-backed plans explained

Green

Green guides you toward a smaller list of 100+ ZeroPoint™ foods that form the basis of healthy eating habits, with a sizeable SmartPoints® Budget to spend on other foods you love. You'll build meals and snacks around these ZeroPoint foods including fruits and veggies, and track other foods that have SmartPoints values.

Blue

Blue guides you toward a list of 200+ ZeroPoint foods that form the basis of healthy eating habits, with a moderate SmartPoints Budget that you can spend on other foods you love. You'll build meals around these ZeroPoints foods including fruits, veggies and lean proteins, and track other foods that have SmartPoints values.

Purple

Purple guides you toward a long list of 300+ ZeroPoint foods that form the basis of healthy eating habits, with a modest SmartPoints Budget that you can spend on other foods you love. You'll build meals around these ZeroPoint foods including fruits, veggies, lean proteins and whole grains, and track other foods that have SmartPoints values.

Meal planning that works

A little bit of forward thinking can take the stress out of daily mealtimes. Here's how to use the weekends to get ahead, and shop smarter to help you stay on track.

Weekend warrior
10 ways to make healthy meals a reality

A few hours at the weekend, or whenever it's convenient for you, can make weekday meals smoother and more efficient. Everyone's schedule and lifestyle is different, so pick and choose strategies that work best for your household.

1 Look at your calendar for the upcoming week. Getting an idea of how many meals you'd like to cook at home, how many lunches you (or your family) might want to take to work or school, and how busy you'll be is an ideal way to start planning.

2 Prepare some meal components. A big batch of grains, a pot of beans, or some homemade tomato sauce can be kept in your fridge or freezer and streamline your weeknight cooking. See our section '8 must-have recipes' on page 34 for some of the DIY staples you can turn to.

3 Plan for leftovers. Do weekends mean you have time for simmering a stew, roasting a whole chicken, or assembling your favourite casserole? Why not double these recipes or make enough so you have at least one go-to meal for later in the week? Freezing is great for soups, stews and casseroles. Roasts like chicken or pork will keep for about three days in the fridge, and you can use them in everything from salads and sandwiches to tacos.

4 Assemble an emergency dinner kit. Don't be caught off guard: stock a corner of your storecupboard with ingredients you can throw together for a healthy meal on the fly. Ideas? Some dry spaghetti, a tin of chickpeas and a tin of water-packed tuna can make a delicious Mediterranean pasta dish with just the addition of garlic, olive oil and maybe a fresh herb (if you have one!). Store all the elements in a kitchen basket for easy retrieval.

5 Think about breakfasts. Imagine how your ideal morning starts, whether it's with a satisfying bowl of Bircher muesli you can enjoy over the morning paper or a savoury muffin you can pack and then eat at the office. Making a few

mornings' meals ahead and refrigerating or freezing them will help keep you on track during the week.

6 Make some spice blends. A roasted chicken breast, a grilled fish fillet, or even baked tofu can make stellar dinner centrepieces with a seasoning blend or rub. Check out our 'Smart seasonings' spread on page 28 for a rundown of spice blends you can mix up quickly at the weekend.

7 Plan for your slow cooker. A slow cooker can make dinner easier to prepare, so make sure you have the ingredients on hand to load it up on your busiest weekdays.

8 Don't forget snacks. Take the time to prepare a few go-to snacks to stash in the fridge or

storecupboard. Cut up long-lasting veggies like carrot, cucumber, and fennel into sticks for dipping into houmous. Prepare a healthy snack like our Fruit & grain snack bars (page 190) to take on the road. And measure and pack up snacks

like nuts, trail mix or baked crisps in small zip-lock bags or containers; mark the SmartPoints value on each to make tracking easier.

9 Visit a farmers' market. Local, in-season produce is usually offered no more than a day or two after it's picked, meaning it's likely to stay fresher throughout the week than supermarket produce. It's also a great way to try new ingredients you might not be familiar with.

10 Enlist a friend. A friend or family member with similar health or cooking goals to you can be an excellent source of support. Make plans to batch-cook together, or agree to each make double of a different recipe and swap the extras with each other.

Shopping
Top tips to make it work for you

Great meals start with great ingredients, so plan to make grocery shopping as enjoyable and stress-free as possible. A few smart strategies will make it easier and keep you on track.

Before you go

Find recipe inspiration. Start by flicking through the chapters of this book, visiting WW.com, and thinking about favourite recipes you can adapt for healthy eating. Gather a few options and make them the starting point for your shopping list. Look online to find out about special offers, especially for in-season produce, at your favourite shops. You may even be able to sign up for alerts to be sent directly to your phone. Plan a few more recipes based around what's economical and seasonal.

Shop with a friend. Go with a friend or family member who shares your health goals or who'd like to split bulk purchases or two-for-one offers to save money. Include a quick stop for coffee or a stroll through a park, or plan to cook or prep together afterward.

Bring your own bags. Sturdy bags with durable handles will make carrying your groceries more comfortable and will protect your food on the way home. Take an insulated bag to keep perishables fresher and frozen items ice-cold.

Commit to your list. Most supermarkets are designed to get you to buy more food, not less or healthier food. That's why planning is essential. Take a list – even if it's only notes on your phone – to keep yourself on track. Online grocery shopping is a great way to stick to your list and not be distracted by supermarket sales tactics.

Don't shop hungry – or thirsty. You'll make better decisions when you aren't distracted by cravings. Make sure you eat before you go shopping and take a bottle of your favourite drink to sip as you shop.

Explore local farmers' markets and speciality stores for great customer service, as well as to get inspired by and connect with your area's local produce and producers.

In the aisles

Start with produce. You may know the formula that half your plate should be devoted to fruits and

vegetables, but have you ever applied that formula to your grocery purchases? If not, start now. Fruits and vegetables should make up about 50 per cent of your trolley or basket. And this is one place where veering off your list is encouraged: if you see an intriguing new fruit or an irresistible display of in-season vegetables, help yourself!

Choose some long-lasting fruits and veggies. Most produce is best when eaten within a few days of purchase, but not all: carrots, cabbage, butternut squash, onions, potatoes, apples, watermelon, beetroot, celery and radishes, to name a few, can last for several weeks when properly stored. Stocking up on these items will give you healthy ingredients to fall back on if you run out of more perishable items.

Take advantage of bulk buys. Grains, beans, nuts, dried fruits and spices are often available in larger packs, making them a bit cheaper in the long run.

Stock up on frozen and tinned foods. Picking up frozen veggies, beans and more ensures you'll always have the makings of a healthy meal. Frozen unsweetened fruits are an affordable luxury when your favourites are out of season, and frozen veg can become speedy sides on busy weeknights. Some of the veggies that hold their quality best when frozen include peas, sweetcorn, carrots, spinach and butternut squash.

Don't forget beverages. Sparkling and infused waters, herbal teas, or even special coffee beans can add variety to your day. Having some of these on hand is a great

weight-loss strategy: a zero SmartPoints drink can often take the place of a snack when you feel like you need a little something.

When you get home
Prep for healthy snacking. Put healthy nibbles out where you can see them: a bowl of fruit on the counter and cut-up vegetables in clear plastic containers at eye level in the fridge are smart options. If you bought nuts or dried fruits, transfer them to single-serving bags and label them with their SmartPoints values for foolproof tracking and portion control.

Keep the momentum going! Seek out more healthy recipes to try, and start planning your next shopping trip. Your cooking and weight-loss successes will make each excursion more rewarding than the last.

Must-have grocery staples

Keeping your storecupboard, fridge and freezer well stocked with basic ingredients will make preparing meals – even at the last minute – a breeze.

Having a well-stocked storecupboard, fridge and freezer is beyond helpful for weight loss, so commit to filling them with the kinds of healthy foods you and your family want. To get started, take an inventory of what you already have on hand. Chances are you have many of the delicious, versatile ingredients used in the tips and recipes throughout this book. Read through our suggestions below and see what makes sense for your WW plan and your lifestyle. As you expand your storecupboard, shopping will take less time each week.

Stock the storecupboard

● Storecupboard items last a long time, so if your budget and storage space allow, create a stash of items such as tinned beans and pulses, chopped tomatoes and passata, light coconut milk, tuna, salmon, and anchovies; dried pasta and noodles; rice and grains; jarred olives, capers and roasted red peppers; and oils and vinegars.
● Go-to basics like breadcrumbs, flour, baking powder, sugar, chilli sauce and dried herbs and spices are essential. If you love Asian-inspired foods, keep a supply of soy sauce, hoisin sauce, curry paste and sesame oil.
● Storecupboard produce basics are the workhorses of the kitchen, so always have onions, potatoes, sweet potatoes, shallots and garlic on hand. Storing them in a basket

in a cool, dark cupboard will help them stay fresh for weeks.
● Convenience foods make cooking healthy meals a possibility when you feel you have no time. As well as the usual tinned tomatoes and beans already mentioned, short-cut ingredients such as pasta sauces and microwave rice and other grains are must-haves for quick meals.
● Nuts are great flavour, texture and nutrient enhancers. Just a sprinkling can take a dish to the next level, so stock a few favourites: almonds, walnuts, pecans, pistachios, hazelnuts, pine nuts and peanuts are all versatile. Seeds like chia, pumpkin, sesame and linseed or ground flaxseed are also terrific, particularly in breakfast dishes. Buy nuts and seeds in small quantities. If storing them for longer than a few weeks, pop them in the freezer. And keep portions small: all nuts and seeds are high in SmartPoints®.

Stock the fridge

● Always keep on hand basics like low-fat milk, yogurt, cheese, eggs, ketchup, mustard, reduced-fat mayonnaise and low-fat spread.
● Weeknight meals call for quick-cooking veg. Buy a few of these each week for recipes and side dishes: asparagus, carrots, peppers, broccoli, Brussels sprouts, cauliflower, green beans, kale, mangetout, spinach and courgettes. For cooking ideas, see 'Make the most of veggies' on page 30.

● Keep a selection of fresh fruits to use in salads and main dishes, and for snacks throughout the day. Apples, pears, kiwis and citrus all keep well and are delicious for snacking and versatile for cooking.
● Fresh herbs will add bright fragrance and flavour and a hit of colour that's not matched by their dried counterparts. Try to keep parsley and one or two other favourite herbs on hand. If you can, grow your own: an outdoor herb garden takes up only a small space, or you can grow herbs indoors in pots near a sunny window.
● Don't forget refrigerated convenience foods, such as prepared pesto, salsa, grated cheese, fresh pasta, pre-washed salad greens, prepped butternut squash and pre-cooked lentils and beetroot.

Stock the freezer

● Keeping a stash of healthy frozen foods means making fewer trips to the supermarket, and if you buy when foods are on offer or in larger packs, you'll save money too. Meats, poultry and seafood spoil quickly in the fridge, so buy a couple of items fresh for early in the week, then rely on foods from the freezer for later in the week.
● Skinless chicken breast fillets, turkey mince, steak, pork loin steaks, fish fillets, prawns and fruits and veggies are great staples for your freezer. Divide them into portions before freezing.

Meals on the go

Taking your own food to work or on outings makes it easier to keep track of the SmartPoints® – and it'll save you money too. Here's some great advice for the perfect packed lunch.

Packing for meals on the go

Out for the day or the evening? Eating at the office or having a family meal at a park is often healthier and more enjoyable when you don't have to rely on restaurants or fast food. It can save you a bundle and tracking can be simpler and more accurate. Here are tried-and-tested strategies to put into your daily and weekly routine.

Start with a plan

Set aside time once a week or so to plan the DIY meals you and your family prefer. Think about what's in season, pull out recipes you'd like to try, and ask other members of your household about what meals they like. Once you've got your ideas together, make a shopping list.

Make the most of leftovers

When cooking, think about doubling your recipe and refrigerating or freezing extras for later. Divide food into individual portions and label them with the dish's name and the SmartPoints value before freezing.

Get the right gear

A paper bag, a simple lunch box or a repurposed takeaway container... these items are all you really need when you want to pack up a meal, but it's both fun and practical to give yourself a few more options. Check out the collection of WW essentials, such as bento boxes, soup mugs and other handy on-the-go food containers, at the WW online shop.

Packing tips and tricks

How to keep that delicious packed lunch (or dinner) in mouthwatering shape? We share our expert tips.

Salads

● Salad travels best in a roomy container, one that won't squash ingredients and that's large enough to seal and shake the whole thing together when you're ready to dress the salad and eat it.
● Pack dressings on the side to keep everything fresh and crisp. A screw-top dressing container is best; consider saving and repurposing a small glass jar (a spice jar or baby-food jar is ideal).
● Got room at your desk to store a few extras? Stock a mini pantry with salt, pepper and soy or chilli sauce to perk up packed lunches.
● Use washable and reusable utensils instead of disposable plastic whenever you can.

Soups and stews

● A vacuum flask will keep soups or stews hot for several hours. A wide-mouth flask is ideal; you can eat out of it instead of having to carry an extra plate or bowl. Ensure food is piping hot when you pack it.
● If a microwave is available, a microwave-safe container with a leak-proof lid is good to carry your meal to work. Keep it chilled before reheating. Remove the lid, cover with a damp sheet of kitchen paper and reheat thoroughly.
● Extras, such as bread, crackers, croutons or tortilla chips, are best kept separate so they stay crisp.
● Wrap delicate toppings like herbs in kitchen paper so they stay moist.

Kitchen equipment

Kitting out your kitchen with the tools that streamline your everyday cooking can be a useful way of helping you create great meals. While they may not all be must-haves, they'll still make life just that little bit easier and can cut recipe preparation time. Here are some tools worth investing in for simpler, healthier cooking.

Baking paper
It's heat-safe and treated so it's nonstick and water-resistant. Use it to line roasting tins or to wrap fish and veggie parcels for oven baking.

Blender or food processor
Each of these will create purées and pastes, which are the basis of many dishes. But if space is tight, choose the one you'll use more often. A blender works best with liquids (think smoothies or soups), while a processor excels at chopping, mincing and slicing ingredients.

Citrus juicer
Fresh lemon or lime juice adds zing to countless dishes.

Griddle pan
A stovetop griddle pan requires little added fat and lets excess drain away.

Knives
You need three: a chef's knife for chopping, a paring knife for precise jobs and a long serrated knife for slicing bread and delicate items such as tomatoes.

Microplane grater
This small grater is ideal for mincing fresh ginger or garlic cloves and finely grating nutmeg or hard cheese.

Muffin tin
Not just for muffins! The individual holes offer built-in portion control for individual frittatas, pies and bakes.

Pestle and mortar
Use this to grind small quantities of seeds, spices and herbs without having to use an appliance.

Steamer
Placed on top of a saucepan on the stove, it lets you cook vegetables, fish and more without added fat.

Wooden spoons
The most basic and most versatile of utensils. Perfect for stirring in a nonstick pan without scratching it.

Zester
This handy gadget is perfect for paring citrus zest in seconds to add flavour to almost any dish – sweet or savoury.

Smart seasonings

Keeping your storecupboard stocked with spices, herbs, and other seasonings means that even a humble chicken breast fillet can taste different every night of the week. Explore this international herb and spice guide to discover 0 SmartPoints® value seasonings, then stock up on the basics you need for your favourite go-to cuisines.

Mediterranean

France
- bay leaves
- Dijon mustard
- herbes de Provence
- rosemary
- shallots
- tarragon
- thyme

Greece
- bay leaves
- dill
- lemon
- garlic
- mint
- oregano

Italy
- balsamic vinegar
- basil
- capers
- oregano
- red pepper flakes
- red wine vinegar
- rosemary
- sage
- thyme

Spain
- oregano
- paprika (smoked, sweet and hot varieties)
- saffron
- sherry vinegar

Asia

China
- chilli
- Chinese five spice
- garlic
- ginger
- rice vinegar
- soy sauce
- star anise
- Szechuan peppercorns

India
- cardamom
- chilli powder
- coriander
- cumin
- curry powder
- garam masala
- ginger
- turmeric

Japan
- ginger
- miso paste
- rice vinegar
- soy sauce
- wasabi paste

Thailand
- coriander
- fish sauce
- fresh chillies
- lemongrass
- lime
- mint
- shallots
- soy sauce
- Thai basil

Middle East
- Aleppo pepper flakes
- cloves
- coriander
- cumin
- mint
- nutmeg
- paprika
- parsley
- preserved lemons
- cardamom
- sumac

Morocco
- cayenne pepper
- cinnamon
- coriander
- cumin
- ginger
- harissa
- preserved lemons
- ras el hanout

South America

Caribbean
- allspice
- bay leaves
- cayenne pepper
- cinnamon
- cloves
- ginger
- hot pepper sauce
- lime
- nutmeg
- Scotch bonnet peppers
- thyme

Mexico
- chilli powder
- chipotle paste
- coriander
- cumin
- fresh chillies
- lime
- oregano

Italian

1 teaspoon dried oregano + 1 teaspoon dried basil + 1 teaspoon dried thyme + 1 teaspoon garlic powder + ½ teaspoon salt + ½ teaspoon dried rosemary, crushed + ¼ teaspoon freshly ground black pepper + a pinch of red pepper flakes

Thai marinade

60ml fish sauce + 3 tablespoons reduced-sodium soy sauce + 2 sliced garlic cloves + 1 sliced stalk lemongrass (white part only) + 8-10 chopped coriander stems; combine all in a food processor.

Mexican

2 teaspoons chilli powder + 2 teaspoons ground cumin + 1 teaspoon dried oregano + 1 teaspoon chilli flakes + 1 teaspoon garlic powder + ½ teaspoon salt

Greek

2 teaspoons dried oregano + 1 teaspoon pared lemon zest + 1 teaspoon dried dill + ½ teaspoon garlic powder + ½ teaspoon salt + ¼ teaspoon freshly ground black pepper

Shortcuts to flavour

We've selected some of the most popular flavour mixes to create some go-to global blends. Each of these will season 4-6 skinless chicken breast or fish fillets. Coat generously, rub in with your hands then use immediately or refrigerate for up to 1 hour before griddling, roasting, stir-frying or pan-frying.

Middle Eastern

2 teaspoons ground cumin + 1 teaspoon freshly ground black pepper + 1 teaspoon ground coriander + 1 teaspoon paprika + ½ teaspoon salt + ¼ teaspoon ground cardamom + a pinch each of ground cloves and ground nutmeg

Make the most of veggies

Most fresh veggies are ZeroPoint™ foods, so you can enjoy as much of these delicious sides as you like. We show you which cooking method works best for the most common veg.

Roasting

Roasting vegetables intensifies flavour and turns otherwise bland veg into something special. Roasted veg is versatile – as well as side dishes, it can be tossed through pasta or puréed to make soups. Put the veg in a nonstick pan and mist with cooking spray or drizzle over a little oil. Roast in a hot oven – 240°C, fan 220°C, gas mark 9 until golden – cook times will vary depending on the veg. Try: Roasted tomato soup on page 104.

Great for roasting:

Artichokes, asparagus, aubergine, beetroot, broccoli, Brussels sprouts, butternut squash, carrots, cauliflower, celeriac, courgettes, fennel, green beans, leafy greens (kale, radicchio, Swiss chard), leeks, mushrooms, onions, parsnips, peppers, potatoes, radishes, swede, spring onions, tomatoes and turnips.

Stir-frying

Like steaming, stir-frying helps retain the colour, flavour and crispness of veg. You'll only need a small amount of oil (use a nonstick wok and add a little water to stop things sticking). Cut different veg into even-size pieces and keep the veg moving in the wok to ensure quick and even cooking. Make sure you don't overload the wok, or the veg will steam. Cook until they're done to your liking – just a few minutes is usually enough. Try: Freekeh stir-fry bowls on page 120.

Great for stir-frying:

Asparagus, aubergine, baby corn, peppers, cabbage (green, red, Savoy), courgettes, fennel, green beans, leafy greens (kale, radicchio, Swiss chard), leeks, mangetout, mushrooms, onions, radishes, spring onions, spinach, sugar snap peas and watercress.

Grilling & griddling

This method will caramelise the natural sugars in vegetables and bring out their flavour without having to add extra ingredients or lots of oil or fat. It's also a speedy way to cook veg. If griddling different veg together, start with firmer ones first, then add delicate ones towards the end. You might find it easier to thread veg onto skewers. Try: Lemon & basil pork skewers on page 114.

Great for grilling & griddling
Asparagus, aubergine, peppers, corn on the cob, courgettes, fennel, mushrooms, onions, spring onions, sugar snap peas and tomatoes (regular, plum and cherry).

Steaming

Steaming vegetables is quick and uses minimal heat and water, which helps preserve many of the nutrients that may be lost when boiling. Steaming veg also retains crispness and colour, so it's a great cooking method when you want really fresh-tasting, colourful dishes. Add seasoning and garnishes like fresh herbs or lemon zest once the veg is cooked. Cook times will vary, depending on how tender you like your veg. Try: Chicken pak choi bowls with miso dressing on page 84.

Great for steaming:
Artichokes, asparagus, broccoli, butternut squash, cabbage (green, red, Savoy), carrots, cauliflower, courgettes, green beans, leafy greens (kale, radicchio, Swiss chard), leeks, mangetout, peas, potatoes, spinach, sugar snap peas and watercress.

About our recipes

While losing weight isn't only about what you eat, we recognise that food plays a critical role in your success and overall good health, and our recipes reflect that…

Our philosophy is simple: to offer recipes that are nutritious as well as delicious. Our recipes are designed to encourage a healthier pattern of eating with lots of ZeroPoint™ foods and lower SmartPoints® value ingredients to make the most of your Budget. Here's how to better understand our recipes and the ingredients that go into them:

Ingredients
Eggs We use medium eggs, unless otherwise stated. Pregnant women, the elderly and children should avoid recipes with eggs which are raw or not fully cooked if not produced under the British Lion code of practice.
Fruit and vegetables Recipes use medium-size fruit and veg, unless otherwise stated.
Reduced-fat soft cheese Where a recipe uses medium-fat soft cheese, we mean a soft cheese with 30 per cent less fat than its full-fat equivalent; where a recipe uses low-fat soft cheese, we mean a soft cheese with 5 per cent fat.
Low-fat spread When a recipe uses a low-fat spread, we mean a spread with a fat content of no more than 39 per cent.

Prep and cook instructions
Prep and cook times These are approximate and meant to be guidelines only. Prep time includes all steps up to and following the main cooking time(s). Stated cook times may vary according to your oven.
Microwaves If we've used a microwave in any of our recipes, the timings will be for an 850-watt microwave oven.

Dietary requirements
Vegetarian recipes Recipes displaying a vegetarian symbol include non-meat ingredients, but may also contain processed products that aren't always vegetarian, such as pesto. If you're a vegetarian, you should ensure you use vegetarian varieties and check the ingredients labels. Where we reference vegetarian Italian-style hard cheese in vegetarian recipes, we mean a cheese similar to Parmesan (which is not vegetarian) but which is suitable for vegetarians.
Vegan recipes Recipes displaying a vegan symbol include no products made from or with the aid of animals or animal products.
Gluten-free recipes Recipes that are labelled as gluten free include ingredients that naturally do not contain gluten, but they may also contain processed products, such as sauces, stock cubes and spice mixes. If so, you should ensure that those products do not include any gluten-containing ingredients (wheat, barley or rye) – these will be highlighted in the ingredients list on the product label. Manufacturers may also indicate whether there is a chance their product may have been accidentally contaminated with gluten during the manufacturing process. For more information and guidance on gluten-free products, visit www.coeliac.org.uk
Nut-free recipes Recipes displaying a nut free symbol include ingredients that do not contain nuts, but may include ingredients produced in facilities that also handle nut products. If you have a nut allergy, check ingredients labels for more information.
Dairy-free recipes Recipes displaying a dairy free symbol include ingredients that naturally do not contain dairy, but may include ingredients produced in facilities that also handle dairy products. If you have a dairy allergy, check ingredients labels for more information.

SmartPoints calculations
SmartPoints values for the recipes in this book are calculated using the values for generic foods, not brands (except where stated). Tracking using branded items may affect the recorded SmartPoints.

When you see these symbols:

Tells you the SmartPoints value per serving for each plan

Note: Recipes conform to the icon designations, but tip and serving suggestions may not.

- Indicates a recipe is gluten free
- Indicates a recipe is vegetarian
- Indicates a recipe is vegan
- Indicates a recipe is nut free
- Indicates a recipe is dairy free

8 must-have recipes

Once you've got these basic recipes under your belt, you'll find making complex dishes becomes a whole lot easier. We've used these in other recipes throughout the book.

Soffritto

makes 4 batches   freezable
prep time 15 minutes
cook time 30 minutes

Use this mix of slowly sautéed veg as a flavour-boosting base for sauces, soups, stews and casseroles.
Heat 2 tablespoons **olive oil** in a very large nonstick frying pan set over a low heat. Finely dice 4 **onions**, 4 **carrots**, and 4 **celery** sticks, then add them to the pan with 4 **fresh bay leaves**. Cook, stirring occasionally, for 20-25 minutes, or until the vegetables are very soft and golden. You may need to add a splash of water if the veg starts to stick. Add 8 sliced **garlic cloves** and cook for a further 2-3 minutes, then remove from the heat and set aside to cool in the pan. Once it's completely cool, divide the soffritto into four equal batches and store in the fridge for up to 5 days, or frozen in an airtight container for up to 6 months. Use this in: Bangers, baked beans & butternut squash bake on page 154, and Tagliatelle tuna puttanesca on page 156.

 2 2 2 SmartPoints value per batch

Tomato sauce

serves 4 (makes 800g)   freezable
prep time 10 minutes
cook time 25 minutes

An easy sauce that's perfect for pasta and pizza.
Put 1 chopped **onion**, 3 roughly chopped **garlic cloves**, 3 tablespoons **tomato purée** and 100ml water into a food processor and blitz to a paste. Mist a large nonstick pan with **calorie controlled cooking spray** and cook the paste over a medium-low heat for 5 minutes. Pour in 680g **passata**, then half-fill the bottle with water and add this to the pan, too. Stir in 2 teaspoons **red wine vinegar**, 2 teaspoons **agave syrup** and 2 teaspoons **dried oregano**, then season and bring to the boil. Reduce the heat and simmer for 20 minutes, until thickened and reduced. Set aside to cool, then store in the fridge for up to 3 days, or freeze in an airtight container for up to 6 months. Use this in: Stuffed pasta shells on page 150, and Chicken parmigiana open sandwiches on page 102.

1 1 1 SmartPoints value per serving

Slow-cooker turkey ragù

serves 4   freezable
prep time 10 minutes
cook time 4 hours 10 minutes

Not just for spaghetti Bolognese, this is a great starting point for lasagne, chilli, cottage pie and much more.
Finely chop 1 **onion**, 1 **carrot** and 1 stick **celery**, then put into a slow cooker with 1 crushed **garlic clove**, 1 teaspoon **dried mixed herbs**, 1 tablespoon **balsamic vinegar** and 2 x 400g tins **chopped tomatoes**, and turn to High. Mist a large nonstick frying pan with **calorie controlled cooking spray** and brown 500g **turkey breast mince** over a high heat for 4-5 minutes. Add the mince to the slow cooker along with 400ml boiling water from the kettle. Put the lid on and cook for 4 hours, until the sauce is thick and reduced. Set aside to cool, then store in the fridge for up to 3 days, or frozen in an airtight container for up to 3 months. To reheat, put into a medium pan and warm over a low heat until piping hot.

2 0 0 SmartPoints value per serving

Two-ingredient pizza dough

makes enough for 2 x 22cm pizzas   freezable
prep time 5 minutes
cook time 15 minutes

This quick, yeast-free dough couldn't be simpler. Use it for pizza or tart bases, or serve it untopped as a flatbread.
Put 180g **0% fat natural Greek yogurt** and 180g **self-raising flour** into a mixing bowl and season well. Mix until a soft dough forms – if it's too dry, add more yogurt, 1 tablespoon at a time, until it's the right consistency. To cook, preheat the oven to 220°C, fan 200°C, gas mark 7 and line 2 baking trays with baking paper. Dust a work surface with 2 teaspoons self-raising flour, then divide the dough into 2 equal pieces and roll out each piece to a 22cm circle. Put onto the prepared trays and bake for 15 minutes until golden. Enjoy as a flatbread or top with your choice of ZeroPoint pizza toppings and bake for another 5 minutes. The baked dough can be wrapped in clingfilm and frozen for up to 1 month. Use this in: Harissa tomato tarts on page 72.

11 10 10 SmartPoints value per pizza base

Homemade sauces, dressings and vegetable stock are a great way to add loads of flavour to other recipes

Vegetable stock

makes 1 litre
prep time 5 minutes
cook time 25 minutes

Homemade stock has loads of natural flavour and is a great way to use up veg that is past its best.
Thickly slice 1 **onion**, and cut 1 large **carrot** and 1 large **celery stick** into 4 pieces each. Put in a stockpot with 1-2 handfuls of leftover **raw vegetables**, cut into large pieces – use firm veg, and avoid potatoes as the starch will make the stock cloudy. Mushrooms, leeks, broccoli, celeriac, swede, turnip and peppers all work well. Add 1 **fresh bay leaf**, a few **herb stalks**, 1 teaspoon **black peppercorns** and 1.25 litres cold water. Bring to the boil, then reduce the heat and simmer, uncovered, for 20 minutes. Strain into a large jug – you should have 1 litre. If you have less, top up with water. If you have more, return the stock to the pan and continue to simmer until it's reduced to 1 litre. Set aside to cool, then store in the fridge for up to 5 days, or freeze in an airtight container for up to 6 months. Use this in: Courgette, lemon & feta risotto on page 152.

0 0 0 SmartPoints value per litre

Vinaigrette

makes 4 x 1 tablespoon servings
prep time 5 minutes

This perfectly-balanced oil and vinegar dressing brings ordinary salad leaves to life.
Put 5 teaspoons **cider vinegar**, 1 tablespoon **extra-virgin olive oil**, ½ teaspoon **English mustard powder**, ½ small crushed **garlic clove** and ¼ teaspoon **herbes de Provence** (or dried mixed herbs) in a clean jar, along with 1 tablespoon water. Season well, then screw on the lid and shake vigorously until combined. Serve drizzled over salads. The vinaigrette can be kept in a sealed container in the fridge for up to 2 weeks. Use this in: Garden greens salad on page 70, Herbed rice salad on page 70 and Tuna Niçoise salad on page 78.

1 1 1 SmartPoints value per serving

Creamy dressing

makes 4 x 2 tablespoon servings
prep time 5 minutes

A creamy, herby dressing made from fat-free yogurt that's great for adding to all kinds of salads and slaws.
Combine 6 tablespoons **fat-free natural yogurt**, the grated zest and juice of 1 **lemon**, 2 teaspoons **white wine or cider vinegar** and ½ teaspoon **onion granules** in a small bowl. Season to taste then stir in 1 tablespoon chopped **fresh soft herbs**, such as chives, flat-leaf parsley, coriander or mint. Serve drizzled over salads. The dressing can be kept in a sealed container in the fridge for up to 3 days. Use this in: Cool coconut yogurt slaw on page 70.

2 0 0 SmartPoints value per serving

Perfect brown rice

serves 4   freezable
prep time 2 minutes
cook time 20-30 minutes

How to cook brown rice to fluffy perfection, every time.
Rinse 225g **brown rice** under cold running water then drain well and transfer to a deep, microwave-safe bowl. Crumble ½ **vegetable stock cube** over the rice, then use your finger tips to rub it through the grains. Pour over 600ml cold water then sit a microwave-safe plate on top of the bowl to cover it completely – ideally with the base of the plate sitting just inside the rim of the bowl. Microwave the rice on High for 20 minutes. Let stand for a further 10 minutes, then remove the plate and fluff up the grains of rice with a fork. To cook on the hob, put the same quantity of rice, stock cube and water in a medium pan with a well-fitting lid. Bring to the boil over a high heat then reduce the heat to a gentle simmer. Cover with a lid and cook for 25 minutes. Remove from the heat and let stand, covered, for 15 minutes. Fluff up the grains with a fork. Cool, then store in the fridge for up to 3 days, or freeze in an airtight container for up to 6 months. To reheat, defrost thoroughly, then follow the same microwave method above, but cook for just 3-4 minutes. Use this in: Herbed rice salad on page 70.

6 6 0 SmartPoints value per serving

Breakfast

Four variations
Toast toppers

Start your day the interesting way by topping your toast with something a little more lavish than the usual spreads.

Double berry jam

serves 1 (jam makes 8 x 1 tablespoon servings)
prep time 5 minutes
cook time 5-10 minutes

To make the jam, put 100g washed, hulled and diced **strawberries** and 50g **blueberries** in a small pan with 2 tablespoons water. Bring to the boil over a medium heat, then simmer for 5 minutes, stirring often, or until the berries have broken down and the mixture is bubbling. Remove from the heat and stir in 1 tablespoon **chia seeds**. Spoon the jam into a small sterilised jar and set aside to cool. Once cool, seal and store in the fridge for up to 5 days, or in the freezer for up to 3 months. To serve, toast 1 slice **WW Soft Malted Danish Bread**, and spread with 1 tablespoon of the jam.

 SmartPoints value per serving
(1 slice of toast with 1 tbsp jam)

Avocado, lime & feta

serves 1
prep time 5 minutes

In a small bowl, roughly mash 80g **avocado** with 1 tablespoon **0% fat natural Greek yogurt** and the juice of ½ **lime**, then season to taste. Toast 1 slice **WW Soft Malted Danish Bread** and spread over the mashed avocado. Crumble over 20g **light feta** and scatter over 1 teaspoon snipped **fresh chives**, then serve.

 SmartPoints value per serving

Tex-Mex tomatoes

serves 4
prep time 5 minutes
cook time 5 minutes

Drain and rinse a 400g tin **pinto beans**, reserving 1 tablespoon of the liquid, then put into a microwave-safe bowl. Add the reserved liquid, 1 teaspoon **cumin seeds**, ½ teaspoon **smoked paprika** and the juice of ½ **lemon**. Mash, then season and cover with the bowl with clingfilm. Put 300g halved **cherry tomatoes** in a microwave-safe bowl with another 1 teaspoon cumin seeds and ¼ chopped **red onion**. Season, then cover the bowl with clingfilm. Microwave the tomatoes on High for 1 minute, then set aside. Microwave the beans on High for 2 minutes, then set aside. Return the tomatoes to the microwave and cook on High for a further 1 minute, then stir in some chopped **fresh coriander**. Toast 4 slices **WW Soft Malted Danish Bread**, and serve topped with the beans, tomatoes and a sprinkling of smoked paprika.

 **SmartPoints value per serving**

Instant croque madame

serves 1
prep time 2 minutes
cook time 5 minutes

Mist a small, nonstick pan with **calorie controlled cooking spray** and set over a medium heat. Add 1 tablespoon water, then crack in 1 **egg**, and cook for 2-3 minutes until the white is set and the yolk soft. Meanwhile heat the grill to medium and toast 1 slice **WW Soft Malted Danish Bread**. Spread with ¼ teaspoon **Dijon mustard** and top with 2 slices **wafer-thin smoked ham** and 1 slice **WW Reduced Fat Cheese**. Grill for 1-2 minutes until the cheese is melted. Top with the fried egg, season to taste and serve.

 SmartPoints value per serving

Green goddess fruit salad

serves 4   **prep time 15 minutes**

Bring a splash of vibrant colour to the breakfast table with this refreshing fruit salad. It's packed with flavour and comes in at just 1 SmartPoint per serving.

2 Granny Smith apples, cored and cut into bite-size pieces

2 kiwi fruit, peeled, halved and thickly sliced

125g white grapes, halved

½ galia melon (or ¼ honeydew melon), seeds and skin removed, and flesh cut into bite-size pieces

Juice of ½ lime

4 large mint leaves, shredded

TO SERVE

4 tablespoons 0% fat natural Greek yogurt

4 teaspoons pumpkin seeds

1   Combine the prepared fruit in a large bowl. Add the lime juice and shredded mint, and stir to combine.

2   Divide the fruit salad between bowls, then serve topped with the yogurt and pumpkin seeds.

1 **1** **1**   SmartPoints value per serving

French-style crumpets

serves 4   prep time 10 minutes   cook time 15 minutes

A very British spin on French toast, these soaked crumpets are the perfect breakfast for a Sunday morning – just add a cuppa, the weekend papers and your choice of fresh fruit.

3 large eggs

2 tablespoons skimmed milk

¼ teaspoon ground cinnamon

8 crumpets

2 teaspoons low-fat spread

TO SERVE

8 teaspoons agave syrup

4 tablespoons fat-free natural yogurt

Prepared fresh fruit (see Cook's tip)

1   Whisk the eggs with the milk and cinnamon in a shallow bowl. Add the crumpets, one at a time, turning a few times to soak up the egg.

2   Melt half the spread in a nonstick frying pan set over a medium heat. Add four of the soaked crumpets and fry for 2-3 minutes on each side until crisp and golden. Remove from the pan and set aside. Repeat with the remaining spread and crumpets.

3   Put two crumpets on each plate, drizzle over the agave syrup and serve topped with the yogurt and fruit.

12   9   9   **SmartPoints value per serving**

Cook's tip
We've used pomegranate, clementines and berries, but you can use any fruit you have to hand for no extra SmartPoints.

Apple & cranberry Bircher muesli

serves 4   **prep time 15 minutes + overnight soaking**

If you're not a morning person, this is the ideal breakfast for you – simple, energising and all the magic happens when you're fast asleep in bed.

120g porridge oats

150g fat-free natural yogurt

3 apples, peeled, cored and grated

1 tablespoon sunflower seeds

1 tablespoon pumpkin seeds

40g dried cranberries

TO SERVE

3 teaspoons chia seeds

1 apple, cored and diced

1   Prepare the muesli the night before you want to serve it. Put the oats into a lidded plastic container. Add the yogurt, grated apples, sunflower and pumpkin seeds, dried cranberries and 150ml water. Stir well to combine. Put the lid on, then chill overnight in the fridge.

2   The next morning, stir the muesli well. If it's too thick, stir in a little more water until it reaches your preferred consistency.

3   Stir 2 teaspoons of the chia seeds into the Bircher muesli, then divide between bowls. Scatter over the remaining chia seeds and the diced apple, then serve.

7   7   3   SmartPoints value per serving

Veggie omelette muffins

serves 4   prep time 10 minutes   cook time 15 minutes

These breakfast sandwiches are an excellent grab-and-go option. Get ahead by chopping all the veg, prepping the eggs as in Step 1, and storing both in the fridge the night before.

6 eggs

2 tablespoons chopped fresh flat-leaf parsley

1½ teaspoons vegetable oil

1 small onion, finely chopped

1 small green pepper, deseeded and finely chopped

100g mushrooms, sliced

4 wholemeal English muffins

4 tablespoons Tomato sauce (see recipe, p34)

1 beef tomato, cut into 4 thick slices

1 In a medium bowl, beat the eggs with the parsley, then season and set aside.

2 Heat ½ teaspoon of the oil in a medium nonstick frying pan set over a medium heat. Add the onion, pepper and mushrooms and cook for 5 minutes, stirring occasionally, until the vegetables are softened. Transfer to a bowl.

3 Heat half the remaining oil in the same frying pan set over a medium heat. Pour in half the egg mixture and tilt the pan so the base is covered. Leave for a minute to allow the eggs to set, then push the cooked edges into the centre using a spatula, letting any uncooked egg run into the gaps. Repeat until the omelette is almost fully set. Top one side of the omelette with half the vegetable mixture. Fold the omelette over the toppings and cook for a further 1 minute. Slide onto a plate and cover to keep warm.

4 Repeat with the remaining oil, eggs and vegetable mixture to make another omelette.

5 Split and toast the English muffins, and cut each omelette in half. Spread the tomato sauce over the base of each muffin, then top with the tomato slices, omelette and remaining muffin halves.

Cook's tip
Want to make this a bit more special? Try adding 40g sliced avocado to each muffin.

11 **8** **8**

8 **5** **5**   SmartPoints value per serving

Eat-your-greens yogurt muffins

makes 12   **freezable**   **prep time 20 minutes**   **cook time 20 minutes**

Make a batch of these muffins – packed with good-for-you ingredients including yogurt, banana, kale and matcha – and you'll have all you need to kick-start 12 healthy mornings.

145g wholemeal flour

140g plain flour

75g granulated sugar

1½ tablespoons matcha powder (optional)

2 teaspoons baking powder

1 teaspoon ground cinnamon

½ teaspoon bicarbonate of soda

½ teaspoon salt

180g fat-free natural yogurt

60ml vegetable oil

2 ripe bananas, thickly sliced

150g kale, stalks removed and leaves roughly shredded

1 large egg

1½ teaspoons vanilla extract

1   Preheat the oven to 180°C, fan 160°C, gas mark 4 and line a 12-hole muffin tin with paper cases.

2   In a large bowl, combine the flours with the sugar, matcha powder (if using), baking powder, cinnamon, bicarbonate of soda and salt. Set aside.

3   Put the yogurt, oil and bananas in a blender and purée until smooth. Add the kale, in batches, and continue to purée until combined. Add the egg and vanilla extract and pulse until just combined. Add the yogurt mixture to the flour mixture, and stir until combined.

4   Spoon the batter into the prepared muffin tin and bake for 20 minutes until risen and golden – a skewer inserted into the centre of the muffins should come out clean.

5   Leave the muffins to cool in the tin for 5 minutes, then transfer to a cooling rack. Serve warm or at room temperature.

The muffins can be stored in an airtight container for up to 3 days or frozen in an airtight container for up to 2 months.

Cook's tip
Turn these muffins into cupcakes by topping them with one quantity of Cheesecake Cream (see recipe, p188), divided between the muffins, and a dusting of ground cinnamon.

6 **5** **5**   SmartPoints value per muffin

Lemon ricotta pancakes

serves 6   prep time 15 minutes   cook time 20 minutes

Creamy ricotta and fluffy whipped egg whites keep these light and airy in texture. They're great for a family breakfast as everyone can help themselves to their favourite toppings.

210g plain flour

1 teaspoon bicarbonate of soda

½ teaspoon salt

230ml buttermilk

100g ricotta

2 eggs, separated

2 tablespoons caster sugar

2 tablespoons finely grated lemon zest, plus extra pared lemon zest to serve (optional)

2 teaspoons vegetable oil

½ teaspoon icing sugar, for dusting

1 Put a large baking sheet in the oven and heat to 140°C, fan 120°C, gas mark 1.

2 In a small bowl, combine the flour, bicarbonate of soda and salt. In a separate bowl, mix together the buttermilk, ricotta, egg yolks, caster sugar and grated lemon zest until combined.

3 Put the egg whites in a clean medium bowl and whisk, using a hand-held electric whisk, until soft peaks form.

4 Gently fold the flour mixture into the buttermilk mixture, until just combined, then fold in the egg whites in two batches.

5 Brush a large nonstick frying pan with a little of the oil and set over a medium heat. Pour 4 ladlefuls of batter into the pan – use about 60ml batter per pancake – and cook for 3 minutes until bubbles appear on the surface. Turn the pancakes and cook for another 2-3 minutes, then remove from the pan and transfer to the baking sheet in the oven to keep warm. Repeat with the remaining oil and batter until you have 12 pancakes.

6 Dust with the icing sugar, then serve 2 pancakes per serving.

Cook's tip

Serve 2 pancakes each, topped with berries, banana and 1 tablespoon 0% fat natural Greek yogurt.

 **SmartPoints value per serving**

Herbed ricotta & bacon frittata

serves 4   prep time 10 minutes   cook time 20 minutes

We like basil and parsley in this easy frittata, but you could use other herb combos, such as chives and dill or mint and coriander – whatever you fancy!

2 teaspoons olive oil

4 unsmoked bacon medallions, cut into thin strips

5 large eggs

60ml semi-skimmed milk

Handful fresh basil leaves, chopped, plus extra leaves to serve

Handful fresh flat-leaf parsley, leaves picked and chopped

120g ricotta

20g Parmesan, grated

1 Preheat the oven to 200°C, fan 180°C, gas mark 6.

2 Heat half the oil in a 22cm ovenproof frying pan over a medium heat. Cook the bacon for 2 minutes, until browned, then remove from the pan and set aside on a plate.

3 In a medium bowl, beat the eggs and milk until combined. Season well, then stir in the bacon, basil and parsley.

4 Heat the remaining oil in the frying pan then pour in the egg mixture. Dot the ricotta evenly over the top and scatter over the Parmesan. Cook for 4-5 minutes over a medium heat until the eggs are starting to set at the edges.

5 Transfer the frying pan to the oven and bake for 10 minutes or until the frittata is set in the centre and the top is browned in places. Remove from the oven and let cool for 5 minutes, then season, scatter over the extra basil and cut into quarters to serve.

Cook's tip

Serve with half a 70g wholemeal English muffin per serving. The recipe will no longer be gluten free.

7 **4** **4**   SmartPoints value per serving

Nutty granola

serves 10   **prep time 5 minutes**   **cook time 20 minutes**

A batch of homemade granola is easy to whip up, and it keeps well so you can easily double the recipe to store and save you time later down the line.

120g porridge oats

25g wheat bran

60g flaked almonds

70g clear honey

½ teaspoon ground cinnamon

45g golden or regular raisins

30g flaxseed

1   Preheat the oven to 180°C, fan 160°C, gas mark 4.

2   Spread the oats and wheat bran on a large baking tray. Bake, stirring often, for 10 minutes until lightly browned.

3   Meanwhile, combine the almonds, honey, cinnamon and a pinch of salt in a large bowl. Add the toasted oat mixture and stir to combine. Spread the mixture back onto the baking sheet and bake, stirring often, for 10 minutes until the mixture is dark golden brown.

4   Transfer to a bowl, then stir in the raisins and flaxseed. Let cool completely before storing in an airtight container.

The granola will keep in an airtight container for up to 2 weeks.

Cook's tip
For a filling breakfast, serve 35g granola per person with a handful of fresh fruit and 150g 0% fat natural Greek yogurt. The recipe will no longer be dairy free.

 SmartPoints value per serving

Poached eggs & bacon with hollandaise sauce

serves 4   prep time 10 minutes   cook time 10 minutes

Make your next portion of eggs Benedict, eggs royale or eggs Florentine healthier than ever with our quick and easy version of hollandaise sauce.

4 eggs

Calorie controlled cooking spray

4 smoked bacon medallions

2 wholemeal English muffins

1 tomato, thickly sliced

2 tablespoons chopped fresh chives

FOR THE HOLLANDAISE SAUCE

50g reduced-fat mayonnaise

60g fat-free natural yogurt

1 teaspoon Dijon mustard

½ teaspoon grated lemon zest

1 teaspoon lemon juice

10g unsalted butter, softened

1. To make the hollandaise sauce, whisk together the mayonnaise, yogurt, mustard and lemon zest and juice in a microwave-safe bowl. Microwave on High for 30 seconds, or until hot. Stir in the butter until melted, then cover to keep warm and set aside.

2. Crack the eggs, one at a time, into a pan of simmering water and poach for about 3 minutes until the whites are just set and the yolks are still soft. Remove from the pan with a slotted spoon and drain on a plate lined with kitchen paper. Cover loosely with kitchen foil to keep warm.

3. Mist a nonstick frying pan with cooking spray and fry the bacon over a medium-high heat for 1 minute on each side until golden.

4. Split and toast the English muffins, then top each muffin half with a slice of tomato, a bacon medallion and a poached egg. Spoon over the hollandaise sauce, then season to taste and serve garnished with the chives.

(7) (5) (5)   SmartPoints value per serving

Cook's tip

This easy hollandaise sauce is also excellent divided between and spooned over 4 x 115g griddled skinless salmon fillets.

(9) (2) (2)

Five-cheese spinach quiche

serves 6   prep time 15 minutes   cook time 35 minutes

Ideal for weekend brunches, crustless quiches are easy to put together and low in SmartPoints, so you can go to town on mouthwatering fillings – like five different cheeses!

Calorie controlled cooking spray

1 teaspoon olive oil

1 small onion, diced

5 large eggs

60ml skimmed milk

1½ teaspoons Dijon mustard

1 teaspoon dried oregano

225g frozen chopped spinach, defrosted and squeezed completely dry

230g ricotta

50g WW Reduced Fat Grated Mature Cheese

50g medium-fat soft goat's cheese, crumbled

50g Gorgonzola or other blue cheese, crumbled

10g vegetarian Italian-style hard cheese, finely grated

1   Preheat the oven to 190°C, fan 170°C, gas mark 5. Mist a 22cm round baking dish with cooking spray.

2   Heat the oil in a large nonstick frying pan over a medium heat. Add the onion and cook, stirring occasionally, for 5 minutes until softened. Remove from the heat and let cool.

3   In a large bowl, whisk together the eggs, milk, mustard and oregano. Season well, then stir in the spinach. Add the ricotta, mature cheese, goat's cheese, Gorgonzola and cooked onion, then stir to combine. Pour the mixture into the prepared baking dish and scatter over the Italian-style hard cheese.

4   Bake for 25-30 minutes, until the quiche is just set and a knife inserted into the centre comes out clean. Set aside to cool for 10 minutes, then cut into wedges to serve.

7 5 5   SmartPoints value per serving

Cook's tip

You can prepare the quiche mixture prior to cooking. Cover and refrigerate, but leave it out at room temperature for 30 minutes so it can warm up enough to keep the baking time the same.

Yogurt breakfast pots

serves 6   prep time 10 minutes

Fresh fruit and yogurt gets a welcome upgrade with a handful of crunchy homemade nutty granola and a swirl of fruity jam. It also makes for a delicious afternoon snack.

90g strawberry jam

900g fat-free natural yogurt

4 large oranges, peeled and segmented

2 bananas, thickly sliced

3 x portions Nutty granola (see recipe, p56)

1   In a bowl, swirl the jam through the yogurt and set aside. In a separate bowl, combine the oranges and bananas.

2   Divide half the fruit mixture between 6 small glasses or bowls, then spoon over half the yogurt mixture. Repeat with the remaining fruit and yogurt. Scatter over the granola, then serve.

8 4 4   **SmartPoints value per serving**

Cook's tip
The pots can be assembled up to 8 hours ahead of serving, so why not get ahead and make them the night before. Add the granola just before serving.

Smoked salmon & egg bagels

makes 4   prep time 10 minutes   cook time 5 minutes

The perfect weekend breakfast: smoked salmon, soft cheese and bagels. We've used bagel thins to keep the SmartPoints low, and shallots, dill and chives to boost the flavour.

90g medium-fat soft cheese

1 shallot, very finely chopped

4 teaspoons chopped fresh dill, plus extra to garnish

1 tablespoon chopped fresh chives, plus extra to garnish

4 eggs, lightly beaten

2 teaspoons vegetable oil

4 x 45g soft seeded bagel thins, split and toasted

120g smoked salmon

1   In a bowl, mix one-third of the soft cheese with the shallot and herbs, then season well. Add the eggs and stir to combine.

2   Heat the oil in a large nonstick frying pan over a medium heat. Pour the egg mixture into the pan and cook, without stirring, for 1 minute until the eggs begin to set. Cook for 3 minutes, until just set, pushing the egg mixture towards the centre of the pan as it cooks. Remove the pan from the heat and set aside.

3   Split and toast the bagel thins, then spread the remaining soft cheese over the bottom halves. Top with the eggs, smoked salmon, extra herbs and remaining bagel thin halves.

9 6 6   **SmartPoints value per bagel**

Recipe builder
Perfect porridge

Warming on a chilly morning and nourishing all year round, a bowl of steaming hot porridge is our favourite go-to breakfast. Once you've mastered the basic recipe, try one of these exciting variations...

Basic porridge

serves 1
prep time 1 minute
cook time 5 minutes

Put 30g **porridge oats** and 160ml **skimmed milk** in a small pan and set over a medium heat. Bring to the boil, then reduce the heat and cook, stirring, for 2-3 minutes until the oats are soft and the mixture is creamy. Serve with a pinch of salt or your favourite sweet topping. You can make the porridge dairy-free and vegan by using oat milk instead – the SmartPoints will remain the same.

5 **5** **2** SmartPoints value per serving

Berry & apple porridge

serves 1
prep time 2 minutes + standing
cook time 5 minutes

Make the basic porridge (see recipe, left), adding ½ small peeled and grated **apple** with the oats and milk. When the porridge is cooked, remove from the heat and scatter over a small handful of **frozen mixed berries**. Cover and set aside for 2 minutes until the berries have completely thawed, then serve with a dusting of **ground cinnamon**.

5 **5** **2** SmartPoints value per serving

Coconut, cardamom & blueberry porridge

serves 1
prep time 2 minutes + standing
cook time 5 minutes

Make the basic porridge (see recipe, far left), using 160ml **Alpro coconut drink** instead of the milk and adding 2 **cardamom pods** that have been squashed with a rolling pin until they've just split open. Once the porridge is cooked, stir in 50g **blueberries** and cook for a further 1 minute until the berries start to soften. Remove and discard the cardamom and serve the porridge with 1 tablespoon Alpro coconut drink drizzled over the top.

5 **5** **2** SmartPoints value per serving

Peanut butter, banana & agave porridge

serves 1
prep time 5 minutes
cook time 5 minutes

Make the basic porridge (see recipe, far left), adding 1 tablespoon **PB Fit peanut butter powder** and ½ mashed **banana** with the oats and milk. Serve the cooked porridge topped with the remaining ½ banana, sliced, 1 tablespoon **0% fat natural Greek yogurt** and 1 teaspoon **agave syrup**.

8 **7** **4** SmartPoints value per serving

Lunch

Four variations
Salads

From side dish to main course, salads are incredibly versatile and varied. Here are four quick and easy recipes that are full of freshness and flavour.

Cool coconut yogurt slaw
serves 4
prep time 15 minutes
cook time 2 minutes

In a dry frying pan set over a medium heat, toast 25g **desiccated coconut** for 1-2 minutes until golden and fragrant. Transfer to a plate to cool. In a large salad bowl, mix the juice of 1 **lime** with 1 quantity **Creamy dressing** (see recipe, p36) until combined. Add 200g shredded **cabbage**, 1 small halved, deseeded and sliced **cucumber**, 2 thinly sliced **celery sticks**, 4 trimmed and shredded **spring onions**, a large handful of chopped **fresh coriander** and 1 teaspoon **nigella seeds** to the bowl. Season to taste and toss to coat. Scatter over the toasted coconut and 1 deseeded and sliced **green chilli** (optional), then serve.

4 **2** **2** SmartPoints value per serving

Roast chicken Waldorf salad
serves 1
prep time 10 minutes

In a medium bowl, toss together a 120g shredded **cooked skinless chicken breast fillet**, 1 small cored and diced **apple**, 1 thinly sliced **celery stick**, 8 halved **white grapes**, ¼ sliced small **red onion** and 20g roughly chopped **walnuts**. Season to taste. Tear 3 **Cos or Romaine lettuce** leaves into bite-size pieces and arrange on a serving plate, then top with the chicken mixture. In a bowl, whisk together 1 tablespoon **reduced-fat mayonnaise**, 1 tablespoon **0% fat natural Greek yogurt**, 1 tablespoon **lemon juice**, 1 teaspoon **white wine vinegar** and ½ teaspoon **dried dill** (or 1 teaspoon chopped fresh dill), until combined, then drizzle over the salad and serve.

8 **5** **5** SmartPoints value per serving

Garden greens salad
serves 1
prep time 10 minutes
cook time 2 minutes

Bring a small pan of water to the boil, add 50g **frozen peas** and cook for 2 minutes, then drain and set aside. In a small bowl, combine 1 tablespoon **Vinaigrette** (see recipe, p36) and 1 teaspoon **elderflower cordial**, then set aside. Tear 1 **Baby Gem lettuce** into bite-size pieces, then scatter over a plate and top with ¼ **cucumber**, halved lengthways, deseeded and sliced, the peas, ½ thinly sliced **celery stick**, 1 trimmed and thinly sliced **spring onion** and a few torn **fresh mint** leaves. Toss to combine, then scatter over a small handful of **salad cress** and serve.

3 **2** **2** SmartPoints value per serving

Herbed rice salad
serves 4
prep time 15 minutes
cook time 2 minutes

Bring a small pan of water to the boil, add 200g **frozen peas** and cook for 2 minutes, then drain and set aside. In a large bowl, combine 300g cooked **Perfect brown rice** (see recipe, p36), 1 trimmed and diced **cucumber**, 1 deseeded and diced **green pepper**, 4 trimmed and thinly sliced **spring onions** and the peas. In a small bowl, whisk together 1 quantity **Vinaigrette** (see recipe, p36), 1 tablespoon **mint sauce** and 1 tablespoon **extra-virgin olive oil**, then drizzle the dressing over the rice mixture. Toss to combine, then mix in a small handful of torn **fresh mint** leaves and a handful of chopped **fresh coriander**. Serve topped with extra mint leaves.

7 **5** **3** SmartPoints value per serving

Harissa tomato tarts

serves 4   prep time 15 minutes   cook time 20 minutes

Delicious served warm or cold, these tarts make the most of juicy, flavoursome tomatoes. Pack them for a picnic, serve them to guests or enjoy them as part of a buffet spread.

2 teaspoons self-raising flour, for dusting

1 quantity Two-ingredient pizza dough (see recipe, p34)

½ small red onion, thinly sliced

4 tomatoes, thickly sliced

4 teaspoons harissa paste

2 teaspoons red wine vinegar

1 teaspoon olive oil

4 tablespoons 0% fat natural Greek yogurt, to serve

1 tablespoon chopped fresh flat-leaf parsley

Rocket, to serve

1 Preheat the oven to 200°C, fan 180°C, gas mark 6, and line 2 baking trays with baking paper.

2 Dust a work surface with the flour. Divide the pizza dough into 4 pieces and roll out each piece to a 15cm circle. Transfer to the prepared baking trays, scatter over the onion then top with the tomato slices.

3 In a small bowl, combine the harissa paste, vinegar and oil, then season well. Drizzle or brush the harissa mixture over the tomato slices, then bake the tarts for 20 minutes until the dough is crisp and golden.

4 Spoon over the yogurt, scatter over the chopped parsley and serve with the rocket on the side.

 SmartPoints value per serving

Black rice salad with smoked tofu

serves 6   **prep time 20 minutes**   **cook time 30 minutes**

A deliciously different salad that is full of ingredients you might not have tried before. Give it a go, you might just find some new favourites.

240g black rice

Calorie controlled cooking spray

500g prepared butternut squash, cut into small cubes

1 teaspoon chopped fresh thyme

200g cavolo nero, stems removed and leaves thinly sliced

225g pack smoked tofu, diced

Seeds of ½ pomegranate

FOR THE SALAD DRESSING

2 tablespoons olive oil

1½ tablespoons red wine vinegar

1½ teaspoons agave syrup

1 small shallot, finely diced

1   Cook the rice to pack instructions, then transfer to a large bowl and set aside to cool.

2   Meanwhile, preheat oven to 220°C, fan 200°C, gas mark 7 and line a large baking tray with kitchen foil. Mist the foil with cooking spray then add the squash and scatter over the thyme. Season well, then mist the squash with cooking spray and roast for 25 minutes, turning once, until tender and golden brown.

3   Meanwhile, mist a large nonstick frying pan with cooking spray and cook the cavolo nero, stirring constantly, for 5-8 minutes or until just starting to soften. You'll need to do this in batches.

4   To make the dressing, whisk together the oil, vinegar and agave syrup in a small bowl, then season to taste and stir in the shallot.

5   In a large bowl, toss together the roasted squash, cavolo nero and rice, drizzle over the dressing and toss again to coat. Gently stir in the smoked tofu, then transfer to a serving platter. Scatter over the pomegranate seeds and serve.

Cook's tip
Make this recipe year-round by using a bag of shredded curly kale instead of the cavolo nero.

7   **6**   **2**   **SmartPoints value per serving**

Turkey meatball & chard soup

serves 8   prep time 15 minutes + soaking   cook time 1 hour 50 minutes

Soaking torn bread in milk before adding it to the turkey mixture ensures the meatballs stay moist and tender, while Parmesan adds a touch of classic Italian flavour.

2 slices WW Thick Sliced Wholemeal bread, crusts removed and bread torn into small pieces

60ml skimmed milk

500g turkey breast mince

40g Parmesan, grated

1 egg

1 shallot, finely chopped

3 tablespoons chopped fresh flat-leaf parsley

1 tablespoon olive oil

1.8 litres chicken stock, made with 2 stock cubes

60g rainbow chard

400g tin cannellini beans, drained and rinsed

1   Combine the bread and milk in a large bowl and set aside for 5 minutes, until the bread is softened. Add the turkey, Parmesan, egg, shallot and 2 tablespoons of the parsley. Season and mix to combine. With damp hands, shape the mince mixture into 24 meatballs (about 2 tablespoons per meatball) and set aside.

2   Heat the oil in a large nonstick frying pan over a medium-high heat. In batches, brown the meatballs for 5 minutes per batch, then remove from the pan and set aside.

3   Pour the chicken stock into a large pan or stockpot and bring to the boil. Add the kale and beans and bring back to the boil. Reduce the heat, add the meatballs and simmer for 1 hour 30 minutes or until the meatballs are cooked through and the soup has thickened slightly.

4   Ladle the soup into bowls and serve garnished with the remaining parsley.

Cook's tip
You'll find rainbow chard in larger supermarkets and in greengrocers, but if you can't get hold of it, use curly kale instead.

4 **2** **2**   SmartPoints value per serving

Tuna Niçoise salad

serves 4   **prep time 10 minutes**   **cook time 10 minutes**

A colourful, filling salad that is easy to rustle up. And if you're cooking for a crowd, you can simply double or triple the quantities.

450g new potatoes, halved or larger ones quartered

200g fine green beans, trimmed

1 small round lettuce, leaves separated

2 x 160g tins tuna in spring water, drained and flaked

2 tablespoons drained capers

8 Kalamata olives, pitted and halved

FOR THE DRESSING

1 quantity Vinaigrette (see recipe, p36)

1 teaspoon Dijon mustard

1   Put the potatoes in a large pan, cover with cold water and bring to the boil. Reduce the heat to medium and cook for 5 minutes. Add the beans and cook for 4 minutes until the potatoes are tender and the beans are cooked but still firm. Drain and transfer to a large bowl.

2   Meanwhile, to make the dressing, put the vinaigrette and mustard in a clean jar. Seal with a tight-fitting lid and shake until combined. Drizzle half the dressing over the potatoes and beans and toss to combine. Add the lettuce to the bowl and toss again to coat.

3   Arrange the dressed salad on a serving platter or in a large salad bowl, then top with the tuna, capers and olives. Drizzle over the remaining dressing and serve.

Cook's tip
Serve the salad with a 65g crusty wholemeal roll per serving. The recipe will no longer be gluten free.

5 **4** **2**   SmartPoints value per serving

Overstuffed sweet potatoes

serves 4   prep time 10 minutes   cook time 10 minutes

If you don't have time for a leisurely lunch, this microwave recipe is a game-changer. Enjoy butter-soft sweet potatoes piled high with spiced veg and cheese in just 20 minutes.

4 x 250g sweet potatoes, scrubbed

2 teaspoons olive oil

1 small red pepper, deseeded and diced

1 small courgette, trimmed and diced

1 large garlic clove, crushed

1 teaspoon ground cumin

200g young leaf spinach

1½ teaspoons chipotle paste

40g light feta, crumbled

1 Pierce the potatoes all over with a fork. Put onto a sheet of kitchen towel in the microwave and cook on High for approximately 8 minutes, until just softened. Remove from the microwave and let cool for 5 minutes.

2 Meanwhile, heat the oil in a large, nonstick frying pan set over a medium-high heat. Cook the pepper and courgette, stirring occasionally, for 5 minutes. Add the garlic and cumin, season well, then cook for 1 minute. Add the spinach, in batches, and cook for a further 1-2 minutes or until the spinach is wilted.

3 When the potatoes are cool enough to handle, cut each one in half, then scoop out the potato flesh, leaving a 1cm-thick shell. Transfer the potato flesh to a medium bowl, stir in the chipotle paste and season to taste. Spoon the potato mixture back into the shells, then top with the vegetables. Scatter over the feta and serve.

Cook's tip
Serve with a mixed green salad dressed with a squeeze of lime juice. The SmartPoints will stay the same.

9 9 1 SmartPoints value per serving

Speedy pizza

makes 1   prep time 5 minutes   cook time 10 minutes

Homemade pizza in under 20 minutes? It's totally possible with
our speedy take on a classic ham-and-cheese pizza.

50g half-fat crème fraîche

**30g WW Reduced Fat Grated
Mature Cheese**

A pinch of English mustard powder

1 WW Wholemeal Wrap

1 shallot, thinly sliced

**2 slices wafer-thin smoked ham,
roughly chopped**

Rocket leaves, to serve

1 Preheat the oven to 200°C, fan 180°C, gas mark 6. In a small
   bowl, combine the crème fraîche, half the cheese and all the
   mustard powder, then season well.

2 Spread the crème fraîche mixture over the wrap, top with the
   shallot and ham, then scatter over the remaining cheese.

3 Transfer to a baking sheet and bake for 7-8 minutes until the
   wrap is crisp and the cheese is melted.

4 Cut into wedges and serve topped with the rocket.

10 10 10   SmartPoints value per pizza

Chicken pak choi bowls with miso dressing

serves 4   **prep time 10 minutes**   **cook time 35 minutes**

Nourishing, filling and adaptable grain bowls are ideal for midweek meals. Poaching keeps the chicken super juicy and tender.

Peeled zest of 1 lemon

½ teaspoon black peppercorns

4 x 165g skinless chicken breast fillets

100g quinoa, rinsed thoroughly

4 baby pak choi, halved lengthways

200g mangetout, halved on the diagonal

1 large carrot, cut into matchsticks

2 teaspoons sesame seeds

FOR THE DRESSING

2 tablespoons rice vinegar

1½ tablespoons white miso paste

2 teaspoons toasted sesame oil

1½ teaspoons clear honey

1½ teaspoons grated fresh ginger

1 teaspoon light soy sauce

1   Put the lemon zest and peppercorns in a medium pan and fill with cold water. Bring the mixture to a simmer over a medium heat, then add the chicken, ensuring it's fully submerged, and cook for 5 minutes. Cover with a lid, remove from the heat and set aside for 30 minutes to poach in the hot liquid until the chicken is cooked through. Transfer the chicken to a plate and set aside.

2   Meanwhile, put the quinoa in a medium pan, cover with 300ml cold water and bring to the boil. Cook for 10 minutes, then reduce the heat, cover and simmer for 20 minutes until the quinoa is tender and all the water has been absorbed. Fluff up the quinoa with a fork and set aside.

3   Steam the pak choi and mangetout in a steamer set over a pan of simmering water for 4-5 minutes, until just tender.

4   While the vegetables are steaming, make the dressing. In a small bowl, whisk together all the dressing ingredients, then set aside.

5   To assemble the chicken bowls, cut the chicken into thick strips. Divide the quinoa between bowls, then top with the chicken, steamed veg and carrot. Drizzle over the dressing and serve garnished with the sesame seeds.

Cook's tip
You can use any vegetable you like in this recipe – just remember to adjust the SmartPoints values, if needed, depending on your plan.

6   **4**   **2**   SmartPoints value per serving

Cheese & leek jacket potatoes

serves 4   prep time 15 minutes   cook time 1 hour 20 minutes

Step away from the baked beans! We've stuffed these fluffy jacket potatoes with a winning combo of eggs, leeks, cheese and chives.

4 x 180g baking potatoes

2 leeks, trimmed, washed and thinly sliced

1 tablespoon low-fat spread

5 large eggs, lightly beaten

80g WW Reduced Fat Grated Mature Cheese

Small handful fresh chives

1   Preheat the oven to 220°C, fan 200°C, gas mark 7. Prick the potatoes all over with a fork and put on a baking tray. Bake for 20 minutes, then reduce the oven temperature to 190°C, fan 170°C, gas mark 5 and bake for another hour until the potatoes are cooked all the way through.

2   Put the leeks and low-fat spread in a nonstick frying pan and set over a medium heat. Cook, stirring occasionally, for 10 minutes or until the leeks are really soft. If you need to, add a splash of water to stop them sticking.

3   Push the leeks to one side of the pan. Pour the eggs into the other side of the pan, increase the heat slightly, and cook, stirring, until the eggs begin to set. When they are half cooked, scatter over the grated cheese and gently fold everything together. When the eggs are completely cooked and the cheese is melted, remove from the heat and season to taste.

4   Split the baked potatoes down the middle and fill with the egg and leek mixture. Snip the chives over the top and serve.

12 9 2   SmartPoints value per serving

Mushroom barley soup

serves 6   prep time 10 minutes + soaking   cook time 40 minutes

This Asian-inspired soup is packed with veggies and pearl barley, making it filling as well as delicious. The white miso paste adds an extra-savoury note to the soup.

25g pack dried shiitake mushrooms

1 tablespoon vegetable oil

3 carrots, sliced

1 onion, finely chopped

3 garlic cloves, crushed

1 tablespoon grated fresh ginger

125g pearl barley

1.5 litres vegetable stock, made using 2 stock cubes

250g pak choi, halved and cut into thick slices

3 tablespoons white miso paste

1 tablespoon lemon juice

1 Put the mushrooms in a heatproof bowl, pour over 500ml boiling water from the kettle and set aside to soak for 20 minutes, until the mushrooms are soft. Remove the mushrooms using a slotted spoon (reserve the soaking liquid), then chop them and set aside.

2 Meanwhile, heat the oil in a large flameproof casserole set over a medium heat. Add the carrots and onion and cook, stirring occasionally, for 5 minutes until softened. Add the garlic and ginger and cook for a further 1 minute.

3 Stir in the pearl barley and chopped mushrooms, then pour in the reserved mushroom soaking liquid and most of the stock (reserve 250ml). Bring to the boil over a high heat, then reduce the heat and simmer, covered, for 30 minutes, until the barley is tender. Stir in the pak choi and simmer for 2 minutes until just soft.

4 Whisk together the miso paste and the reserved vegetable stock until smooth, then add this to the soup along with the lemon juice. Ladle into bowls and serve.

Cook's tip
Serve the soup garnished with some sliced spring onions. The SmartPoints will stay the same.

4 **4** **4** SmartPoints value per serving

Salmon, mint & cucumber baguettes

makes 4   prep time 10 minutes   cook time 10 minutes

So simple, but so delicious. This richly flavoured salmon filling is perfect to put in a crusty baguette, and makes a great packed lunch for work or a day spent out and about.

2 x 150g part-baked brown baguettes (we used Sainsbury's)

213g tin pink salmon, drained

½ cucumber, finely diced

½ red onion, finely diced

9 Kalamata olives, pitted and chopped

3 tablespoons 0% fat natural Greek yogurt

2 tablespoons chopped fresh mint

Grated zest and juice of 1 large lime

½ teaspoon sriracha sauce

4 Ruby Gem lettuce leaves

2 tomatoes, thickly sliced

1 Preheat the oven to 220°C, fan 200°C, gas mark 7, then bake the baguettes to pack instructions.

2 Use a fork to flake the salmon into a medium bowl. Add the cucumber, onion, olives, yogurt, mint, lime zest and juice, and sriracha, then season to taste.

3 Halve the baguettes, then split and fill with the lettuce and tomato. Spoon over the salmon mixture and serve.

8 7 7   **SmartPoints value per baguette**

Harissa prawn cocktail

serves 1   prep time 15 minutes

Juicy prawns, refreshing cucumber ribbons, crisp lettuce and a low SmartPoints spicy tomato mayo combine to make the perfect modern take on the prawn cocktail.

1 Baby Gem lettuce, or ¼ small iceberg lettuce, shredded

¼ cucumber, peeled into ribbons using a vegetable peeler

125g cooked and peeled prawns

Lemon wedges, to serve

FOR THE COCKTAIL SAUCE

1 teaspoon tomato purée

1 tablespoon reduced-fat mayonnaise

1 tablespoon fat-free natural yogurt

2 teaspoons lemon juice

½ teaspoon harissa paste

Pinch of sweet paprika, plus extra to serve

1 In a small bowl, combine all the sauce ingredients, season to taste and set aside.

2 Arrange the shredded lettuce and cucumber ribbons on a plate. In a small bowl, combine the prawns with 2 teaspoons of the sauce, then pile them on top of the salad. Scatter over the extra paprika and serve with the remaining sauce and the lemon wedges on the side.

3 **1** **1**   SmartPoints value per serving

Buffalo-style chicken salad

serves 4   prep time 15 minutes   cook time 10 minutes

If you love buffalo chicken wings, then this is the salad for you.
It has all the classic spicy flavour, but it's much lower in fat.

Calorie controlled cooking spray

500g chicken breast mini fillets
(you'll need 12)

2 teaspoons Tabasco sauce

1 Romaine lettuce, shredded

½ small cucumber, diced

2 sticks celery, thinly sliced
(leaves reserved)

2 spring onions, trimmed and
thinly sliced

1 red pepper, deseeded and diced

1 carrot, diced

50g Stilton, crumbled

FOR THE SPICE RUB

½ teaspoon hot smoked paprika

½ teaspoon ground cumin

¼ teaspoon chilli powder

½ teaspoon salt

FOR THE DRESSING

1½ tablespoons extra-virgin olive oil

2 tablespoons red wine vinegar

1 garlic clove, crushed

1 In a small bowl, combine all the spice rub ingredients then
season with freshly ground black pepper. Rub the spice mixture
over the chicken fillets and set aside.

2 To make the dressing, whisk together the dressing ingredients,
then season to taste and set aside.

3 Mist a large nonstick frying pan with cooking spray and set over
a medium-high heat. Griddle the chicken for 4 minutes on each
side, until cooked through. Transfer to a plate, drizzle over the
Tabasco sauce and turn to coat.

4 To assemble the salad, put the lettuce, cucumber, celery,
spring onions, pepper and carrot in a large bowl. Drizzle over
the dressing and toss to coat. Transfer to a large serving
platter, then scatter over the chicken and serve topped with
the reserved celery leaves and the Stilton.

5 **4** **4** SmartPoints value per serving

Cook's tip
Bulk up the salad by
adding 185g cooked
quinoa per serving.

11 **10** **4**

Salmon, white bean & pasta salad

serves 4   prep time 15 minutes   cook time 5 minutes

A storecupboard recipe that makes an effortlessly delicious lunch in next to no time. Ideal for taking to work as it can be served warm or cold and transports well.

**120g fresh chickpea fusilli
(see Cook's tip)**

**80ml chicken stock, made with
½ stock cube**

60ml red wine vinegar

1½ tablespoons olive oil

1 tablespoon finely grated lemon zest

**400g tin cannellini beans, drained
and rinsed**

213g tin pink salmon, drained

**250g jar roasted red peppers in brine,
drained and chopped**

1 small red onion, chopped

4 teaspoons drained capers

**Handful fresh flat-leaf parsley
leaves, to serve**

1   Bring a large pan of water to the boil, add the pasta and cook to pack instructions, until al dente. Drain and cool under cold running water, then drain again and set aside.

2   Whisk together the chicken stock, vinegar, oil and lemon zest in a large bowl. Season, then add the cooked pasta, beans, salmon, roasted pepper, onion and capers and toss to combine.

3   Divide between bowls and serve garnished with the parsley.

7 5 2   SmartPoints value per serving

Cook's tip
If you can't find chickpea pasta, you can use wholewheat pasta instead (this is not gluten free). The SmartPoints will stay the same.

Mexican-style chicken soup

serves 4   freezable   prep time 10 minutes   cook time 30 minutes

Some classic Mexican ingredients – peppers, chilli, lime, sweetcorn and avocado – give this soup plenty of bold flavour.

2 teaspoons olive oil

500g skinless chicken breast fillets, cut into bite-size pieces

1 onion, chopped

1 small green pepper, deseeded and chopped

1 small green chilli, deseeded and chopped

2 garlic cloves, crushed

1 tablespoon mild chilli powder

2 teaspoons ground cumin

850ml chicken stock, made with 1 stock cube

400g tin chopped tomatoes

340g tin sweetcorn, drained

1 tablespoon freshly squeezed lime juice, plus wedges to serve

80g avocado, diced, to serve

Small handful coriander leaves, chopped, to serve

1   Heat half the oil in a large nonstick pan and brown the chicken over a medium-high heat for 5 minutes, stirring often. Season, then transfer to a plate.

2   Heat the remaining oil in the pan and fry the onion, pepper and chilli for 5 minutes until softened. Add the garlic, chilli powder and cumin and cook, stirring constantly, for 1 minute. Pour in the stock, then add the tomatoes and sweetcorn. Cover and bring to the boil.

3   Reduce the heat to low and simmer, covered, for 10 minutes until the vegetables are tender. Return the chicken to the pan and simmer for 5 minutes, until cooked through. Remove from the heat and stir in the lime juice.

4   Ladle the soup into bowls, top with the avocado and coriander and serve with the lime wedges on the side.

The soup (minus the avocado and coriander garnish) can be frozen in an airtight container for up to 3 months.

Cook's tip

While the soup is cooking, cut a WW White Wrap into 8 triangles. Mist a large baking tray with calorie controlled cooking spray, scatter over the wrap pieces and bake at 200°C, fan 180°C, gas mark 6, for 3-4 minutes until crisp. Crumble over the soup to serve. The recipe will no longer be gluten free.

 SmartPoints value per serving

6   3   3

7   3   3

Courgette ribbons with mixed herb pesto & tomatoes

serves 4   prep time 20 minutes

An Italian-style mixed-herb pesto transforms this fresh tomato and courgette salad into something really special.

450g tomatoes, diced

200g courgettes, peeled into ribbons using a vegetable peeler

20g vegetarian Italian-style hard cheese, grated, to serve

FOR THE HERB PESTO

25g fresh basil leaves

10g fresh flat-leaf parsley, leaves picked

10g fresh coriander, leaves picked

10g fresh chives, chopped

1 garlic clove, crushed

4 teaspoons extra-virgin olive oil

20g vegetarian Italian-style hard cheese, grated

1 Put the diced tomatoes into a sieve set over a medium bowl to allow the tomato water to drain.

2 Meanwhile, make the herb pesto. Put the herbs, garlic and 60ml cold water into a food processor and pulse until finely chopped. With the motor still running, gradually add the oil and continue to process until the mixture forms a coarse purée. Transfer to a small bowl and stir in the grated cheese. Season to taste and set aside. If the mixture is too thick, thin it out with a little of the drained tomato water.

3 Loosely pile the courgette ribbons onto 4 plates. Scatter over the tomatoes and spoon over the pesto. Season and serve garnished with the grated cheese.

3 3 3 SmartPoints value per serving

Chicken parmigiana open sandwiches

makes 4   prep time 10 minutes   cook time 40 minutes

This version of the classic Italian dish features crisp, crumbed chicken breast topped with our easy tomato sauce and two cheeses, and served on toasted sourdough bread.

1½ tablespoons red wine vinegar

1 tablespoon extra-virgin olive oil

1 large garlic clove, crushed

¼ teaspoon dried oregano

70g panko breadcrumbs

4 x 125g skinless chicken breast fillets

Calorie controlled cooking spray

¼ quantity (you'll need about 120g) Tomato sauce (see recipe, p34)

40g light mozzarella, grated

20g Parmesan, grated

4 x 50g slices sourdough bread

Rocket leaves, to serve

Pinch chilli flakes, to serve

1 In a large shallow bowl, whisk together the vinegar, oil, garlic, oregano and 1 tablespoon water, then season well. Spread the breadcrumbs on a sheet of greaseproof paper.

2 Put the chicken between 2 pieces of clingfilm and flatten with a rolling pin to a thickness of approximately 1cm. Dip 1 chicken fillet in the vinegar mixture, turning to coat, then press into the crumbs, turning to coat. Repeat with the remaining chicken.

3 Preheat the oven to 200°C, fan 180°C, gas mark 6. Mist a large nonstick frying pan with cooking spray and set over a medium heat. Cook the chicken, in batches, for 3 minutes on each side, then transfer to a baking tray. Bake for 15 minutes, then spoon the tomato sauce over the centre of the chicken and scatter over the mozzarella and Parmesan. Bake for 10 minutes until the chicken is cooked through and the cheese is melted.

4 Toast the bread and divide between plates. Top with the rocket followed by the chicken parmigiana. Scatter over the chilli flakes and serve.

9   8   8   SmartPoints value per sandwich

Recipe builder
Soups

Homemade tomato soup is a cinch to make and is often lower in SmartPoints than any tinned variety. Plus, it makes a great base for other soups – just add extra ingredients.

Roasted tomato soup
serves 4   freezable
prep time 15 minutes
cook time 30 minutes

Preheat the oven to 190°C, fan 170°C, gas mark 5. Thickly slice 1 **onion** and arrange in a single layer in a large roasting tin. Scatter over 2 thinly sliced **carrots** and 800g halved or quartered **mixed tomatoes**, then nestle 2 unpeeled **garlic cloves** and 2 sprigs **fresh thyme** among the veg. Season, drizzle over 1 tablespoon **olive oil** and roast for 30 minutes until the onion is tender. Remove and discard the thyme, and transfer all the veg to a large pan. Squeeze the garlic flesh from the skins and add to the pan along with 650ml vegetable stock (made with 2 **stock cubes**), 2 tablespoons **tomato purée** and 1 teaspoon **balsamic vinegar**. Bring the mixture to a simmer, then remove from the heat. Using a stick blender, blitz the soup until smooth, then ladle into bowls and serve garnished with fresh thyme leaves. The soup can be frozen in an airtight container for up to 3 months.

2 **2** **2** SmartPoints value per serving

Virgin Mary gazpacho
serves 4   freezable
prep time 15 minutes
cook time 30 minutes

Make a batch of **Roasted tomato soup** (see recipe, left), omitting the balsamic vinegar. Stir in 2 teaspoons **Worcestershire sauce**, the juice of ½ **lemon**, and 1 teaspoon **Tabasco sauce**, then transfer to a large jug and chill in the fridge until ready to serve. Ladle the soup into bowls, scatter over 1 thinly sliced **celery stick** and a few **celery leaves**, then season and serve with **lemon wedges** on the side. If it's a hot day, add some ice cubes to the soup when serving. The soup can be frozen in an airtight container for up to 3 months.

2 **2** **2** SmartPoints value per serving

Harissa, butter bean & roasted tomato soup

serves 4   freezable
prep time 15 minutes
cook time 35 minutes

Make a batch of **Roasted tomato soup** (see recipe, far left), and set over a medium-low heat. Add 4 teaspoons **harissa paste**, then blitz with a stick blender to combine. Stir 2 x 400g tins drained and rinsed **butter beans** into the soup, then heat through. Serve topped with 4 tablespoons **fat-free natural yogurt**. The soup can be frozen in an airtight container for up to 3 months.

6 2 2   SmartPoints value per serving

Mediterranean-style roasted tomato & pepper soup

serves 4   freezable
prep time 15 minutes
cook time 35 minutes

Make a batch of **Roasted tomato soup** (see recipe, far left), and set over a medium-low heat. Drain a 450g jar **roasted red peppers in brine**, and add half to the soup, along with a small handful **fresh basil**, then blitz with a stick blender until smooth. Dice the remaining red peppers and stir them into the soup, then heat through. Serve the soup topped with 25g sliced **pitted black olives** and some more fresh basil leaves. The soup can be frozen in an airtight container for up to 3 months.

2 2 2   SmartPoints value per serving

Dinner

Four variations
Skinless chicken breast fillets

Simple to cook, delicious and versatile, skinless chicken breast fillets are the ideal ingredient for a quick and easy dinner.

Herb-roasted chicken

serves 4
prep time 5 minutes
cook time 20 minutes

Preheat the oven to 200°C, fan 180°C, gas mark 6. Put 1 tablespoon **olive oil** in a pan with 2 halved **garlic cloves** and warm over a medium heat for 2 minutes to infuse. Increase the heat to high, remove the garlic and reserve. Season 4 x 165g **skinless chicken breast fillets**, then add to the pan. Cook for 1 minute on each side, then transfer to a baking dish. Remove the pan from the heat and add 2 tablespoons water. Swirl to combine with the chicken juices, then pour over the chicken. Squeeze over the juice of 1 **lemon**, then scatter over 1 teaspoon **dried sage**, 1 tablespoon chopped **fresh flat-leaf parsley** and some **fresh thyme sprigs**. Add the reserved garlic, then roast for 15 minutes until cooked through. Serve with **Herbed rice salad** (see recipe, p70).

10 **7** **4** SmartPoints value per serving

Kiev-style chicken

serves 4
prep time 5 minutes
cook time 20 minutes

Preheat the oven to 200°C, fan 180°C, gas mark 6. Grate a 125g ball of **light mozzarella**, then mix with 4 tablespoons **medium-fat soft cheese**, 4 crushed **garlic cloves** and a handful chopped **fresh flat-leaf parsley** leaves, and season well. Cut pockets in the sides of 4 x 165g **skinless chicken breast fillets**, so you can open each fillet like a book but the ends are still joined. Push half of the filling inside each fillet. Mist with **calorie controlled cooking spray**, scatter each fillet with 1 tablespoon **panko breadcrumbs**, mist again with more cooking spray, then transfer to a baking tray. Bake for 20 minutes until the chicken is cooked through and the crumb is golden. Serve with **Garden greens salad** (see recipe, p70).

9 **6** **6** SmartPoints value per serving

Spiced roast chicken

serves 4
prep time 5 minutes
cook time 20 minutes

Preheat the oven to 200°C, fan 180°C, gas mark 6. Season 4 x 165g **skinless chicken breast fillets** and cut slashes across the tops. In a small bowl, combine 2 tablespoons **lemon juice**, 2 teaspoons **sunflower oil**, 2 tablespoons **0% fat natural Greek yogurt**, 2 crushed **garlic cloves**, 1 teaspoon **curry powder**, 1 teaspoon **ground turmeric** and 1 teaspoon **ground cumin**. Rub the mixture all over the chicken, then transfer to a baking dish and roast for 20 minutes, until cooked through. Serve with **Cool coconut yogurt slaw** (see recipe, p70).

6 **3** **3** SmartPoints value per serving

Honey-mustard baked chicken

serves 4
prep time 10 minutes
cook time 20 minutes

Preheat the oven to 200°C, fan 180°C, gas mark 6. In a small bowl, combine 1 tablespoon **wholegrain mustard** with 1 teaspoon **Dijon mustard**, 1 tablespoon **clear honey**, 1 teaspoon **dried sage** and the grated zest of ½ **orange**. Season, then brush over 4 x 165g **skinless chicken breast fillets**. In a separate small bowl, mix 100ml chicken stock (made with ½ **stock cube**), 1 teaspoon wholegrain mustard, the juice of ½ **orange** and 1 teaspoon **cider vinegar**. Put the chicken fillets into a baking dish, pour in the stock mixture, then bake for 20 minutes until cooked through. Serve with steamed ZeroPoint vegetables.

4 **3** **3** SmartPoints value per serving

Katsu fish with rice & shredded salad

serves 4   **prep time 25 minutes**   **cook time 35 minutes**

A popular Japanese dish, katsu is usually made with crumbed chicken or pork, but we've come up with this delicious fish version.

40g plain flour

1 egg, lightly beaten

75g panko breadcrumbs

4 x 120g firm white skinless fish fillets – such as cod, pollock or haddock

Calorie controlled cooking spray

1 quantity Perfect brown rice (see recipe, p36), to serve

FOR THE CURRY SAUCE

Calorie controlled cooking spray

2 onions, diced

2 carrots, diced

2 garlic cloves, crushed

1 tablespoon grated fresh ginger

4 teaspoons mild curry powder

1 teaspoon ground turmeric

400ml Alpro coconut milk drink

FOR THE SHREDDED SALAD

4 spring onions, trimmed and shredded

½ cucumber, halved, deseeded and shredded

125g mangetout, very finely sliced

1 yellow pepper, deseeded and very finely sliced

Juice of ½ lime

1   To make the curry sauce, mist a deep, nonstick pan with cooking spray and cook the onions and carrots over a medium heat for 8-10 minutes until soft and starting to turn golden. Add a splash of water if the vegetables start to stick.

2   Stir in the garlic and ginger and cook for 1 minute, then add the curry powder and turmeric and stir to combine. Pour in the coconut milk drink and 150ml water. Bring to a simmer, then cover, reduce the heat to low and cook for 20 minutes or until the carrots are soft. Blitz to a sauce using a hand-held stick blender or food processor. Season to taste and set aside.

3   While the sauce is cooking, preheat the oven to 200°C, fan 180°C, gas mark 6 and line a baking tray with baking paper. Put the flour on a plate and season well. Put the egg and breadcrumbs on separate plates. Dust each fish fillet in the flour, then dip in the egg and coat in the crumbs. Arrange the fish on the prepared baking tray then mist with cooking spray. Bake for 18 minutes until the fish is cooked through and the breadcrumbs are golden.

4   To make the shredded salad, toss together all the salad ingredients in a large bowl until well combined.

5   Spoon the curry sauce onto plates, then top with the crumbed fish fillets. Serve with the rice and salad on the side.

11 **10** **4**   **SmartPoints value per serving**

Garlicky kale & bean stuffed potatoes

serves 4   prep time 20 minutes   cook time 1 hour 5 minutes

These double-baked potatoes are filled with a delicious combination of red pepper, onion, beans and curly kale, plus garlic and fresh thyme for extra flavour.

4 x 220g baking potatoes

2 teaspoons olive oil

1 red pepper, deseeded and thinly sliced

1 red onion, halved and cut into thin wedges

2 teaspoons fresh thyme leaves

2 garlic cloves, sliced

120g shredded curly kale

400g tin cannellini beans, drained and rinsed

80ml vegetable stock, made using ½ stock cube

1 tablespoon low-fat spread

1   Preheat the oven to 200°C, fan 180°C, gas mark 6. Prick the potatoes all over with a fork and put on a baking tray. Bake for 1 hour, until tender, then set aside to cool slightly.

2   Meanwhile, heat the oil in a large nonstick frying pan over a medium heat. Cook the pepper, onion, thyme and garlic, stirring, for 10 minutes, until the vegetables are very soft. Add the kale and cook, stirring, for 5 minutes, until wilted, adding a splash of water if the mixture starts to dry out. Keep warm.

3   Reserve 90g of the beans and put the rest into a food processor. Blitz until smooth, then transfer to a medium bowl.

4   When the potatoes are cool enough to handle, cut them in half, lengthwise. Scoop out the potato flesh, leaving a 1cm-thick shell. Put the potato flesh in the bowl with the puréed beans, then mash with a fork until combined. Stir in the stock and low-fat spread, then season to taste. Spoon the mixture back into the potato shells and return to the baking tray. Bake for 5 minutes, until heated through.

5   Stir the reserved beans through the vegetable mixture. Season to taste, pile the mixture onto the potatoes, then serve.

12   10   1   **SmartPoints value per serving**

Lemon & basil pork skewers

serves 4   **prep time 15 minutes + marinating**   **cook time 15 minutes**

These colourful kebabs combine delicious garden veg with cubes of tender marinated lean pork for a tasty dinner the whole family will enjoy.

Finely grated zest and juice of 1 lemon, plus lemon wedges to serve

4 teaspoons vegetable oil

3 garlic cloves, crushed

4 x 120g lean pork loin steaks, diced

1 courgette, halved lengthways and thickly sliced

1 yellow courgette (see Cook's tips), halved lengthways and thickly sliced

8 baby plum or cherry tomatoes

1 red onion, halved then each half cut into 8 wedges

Large handful chopped fresh basil

Calorie controlled cooking spray

Cook's tips
If you can't find yellow courgettes, simply use 2 green courgettes instead. Serve with 75g cooked couscous per serving, if you like. The recipe will no longer be gluten free.

1   In a large bowl, combine the lemon zest, lemon juice, oil and garlic, then season well. Add the pork, courgettes, tomatoes, onion and half the basil, then toss to coat. Set aside to marinate for 10 minutes.

2   Thread the pork and vegetables onto 8 long metal skewers (if using bamboo skewers, soak them in cold water for 30 minutes beforehand to prevent them burning), reserving any marinade.

3   Preheat the oven to 180°C, fan 160°C, gas mark 4. Mist a large nonstick griddle pan with cooking spray and set over a medium-high heat.

4   Griddle the skewers for 5 minutes, turning frequently, until the pork and vegetables are lightly charred. Transfer the skewers to a baking tray, brush over any reserved marinade and bake for 10 minutes, until the pork is cooked through.

5   Transfer the skewers to a serving platter, scatter over the remaining basil and serve with the lemon wedges.

 SmartPoints value per serving

Peruvian-style roast chicken with green sauce & avocado salad

serves 6   prep time 20 minutes + resting   cook time 1 hour

The spice rub really takes the flavour in this dish to another level, while the green chilli sauce adds a fiery freshness.

Calorie controlled cooking spray

2 tablespoons white wine vinegar

1 tablespoon paprika

1 tablespoon ground cumin

5 garlic cloves, crushed

2 teaspoons vegetable oil

1¾ teaspoons salt

¼ teaspoon cayenne pepper

1.5kg whole chicken, skin removed

Lime wedges, for serving

FOR THE GREEN SAUCE

30g coriander, leaves picked

2 small green chillies, roughly chopped

2 spring onions, trimmed and chopped

1 garlic clove, halved

1 tablespoon white wine vinegar

Juice of 1 lime

4 tablespoons reduced-fat mayonnaise

FOR THE AVOCADO SALAD

1 Romaine lettuce, shredded

½ red onion, finely sliced

1 avocado, peeled, stone removed, and thinly sliced

Juice of ½ lime

1 Preheat the oven to 200°C, fan 180°C, gas mark 6. Mist a roasting rack with cooking spray and put in a roasting tin.

2 In a small bowl, combine the vinegar, paprika, cumin, garlic, oil, salt and cayenne pepper. Make a few slits in the thickest part of the chicken, then rub the spice mixture all over the chicken and inside its cavity. Put the chicken, breast-side up, on the prepared rack and roast for 1 hour or until cooked through. Remove from the oven and set aside to rest for 10 minutes.

3 Meanwhile, make the sauce and salad. For the sauce, put all the ingredients into a food processor and blend until smooth. Season to taste. For the salad, combine the lettuce and onion in a salad bowl, top with the avocado and sprinkle over the lime juice. Season to taste.

4 Put the chicken onto a platter, before carving at the table. Serve with the salad, sauce and lime wedges on the side.

8 **8** **8**   SmartPoints value per serving

Sage & blue cheese chicken burgers

serves 4   prep time 15 minutes   cook time 10 minutes

Shredded apple, onion and sage keeps these lean chicken burgers juicy, as well as adding loads of flavour. The blue cheese dressing is the perfect finishing touch.

500g skinless chicken breast fillets

1 red apple, peeled, cored and grated

1 small red onion, grated

15g panko breadcrumbs

1 tablespoon chopped fresh sage

1 tablespoon Tabasco sauce

1 tablespoon Worcestershire sauce

Calorie controlled cooking spray

4 x 60g wholemeal burger buns

4 round lettuce leaves

1 tomato, thinly sliced

FOR THE BLUE CHEESE DRESSING

40g Gorgonzola or other blue cheese, broken into small pieces

2 tablespoons buttermilk

2 teaspoons reduced-fat mayonnaise

1 Put the chicken into a food processor and pulse until very finely chopped. Transfer to a bowl, then add the apple, onion, breadcrumbs, sage, Tabasco sauce and Worcestershire sauce. Season, then shape the mixture into 4 patties.

2 Heat a large nonstick griddle pan over a medium heat. Mist the patties all over with cooking spray and griddle for 4-5 minutes on each side, or until the chicken is cooked through.

3 Meanwhile, to make the blue cheese dressing, combine the Gorgonzola, buttermilk and mayonnaise in a small bowl, then season to taste.

4 To assemble the burgers, split and toast the buns, then spoon the dressing over the base of each bun. Top with the chicken burgers, lettuce, tomato and remaining bun halves, then serve.

8 7 7   **SmartPoints value per serving**

Cook's tip

Serve with butternut squash wedges on the side, for no extra SmartPoints. Preheat the oven to 200°C, fan 180°C, gas mark 6. Cut 1 peeled and deseeded butternut squash into wedges, put on a baking tray and mist with calorie controlled cooking spray. Season and bake for 25 minutes, or until crisp and golden.

Freekeh stir-fry bowls

serves 4   **prep time 10 minutes**   **cook time 30 minutes**

Nutty-tasting freekeh is a great alternative to rice and can be used in the same sorts of dishes. This recipe is a take on egg fried rice and makes a tasty all-in-one dinner.

200g freekeh

4 eggs

4 tablespoons chopped fresh coriander

4 teaspoons groundnut oil

3 spring onions, trimmed and finely sliced, plus extra to serve

3 garlic cloves, crushed

2 tablespoons grated fresh ginger

150g sugar snap peas, trimmed and halved

200g small broccoli florets

1 red pepper, deseeded and diced

2 tablespoons light soy sauce

4 teaspoons sriracha sauce, to serve (optional)

Lime wedges, to serve

1   Put the freekeh, 625ml cold water and a pinch of salt into a small pan and bring to the boil over a high heat. Reduce the heat to low and simmer, covered, for 25 minutes, until the freekeh is tender but still has some bite. Drain, then rinse under cold running water and drain again.

2   Meanwhile, in a small bowl, whisk together the eggs and half the coriander. Season well.

3   Heat 1 teaspoon of the oil in a large nonstick wok or frying pan set over a high heat. Add the egg mixture and swirl to coat the pan. Stir-fry for 1 minute, until set, then transfer to a small bowl and set aside.

4   Heat the remaining oil in the wok then stir-fry the spring onions, garlic and ginger for 30 seconds, until fragrant. Add the sugar snap peas, broccoli and pepper to the wok and stir-fry for 3-5 minutes, until the sugar snap peas and broccoli are bright green. Reduce the heat to medium and add the freekeh and soy sauce. Stir fry for 2-3 minutes, until hot.

5   Divide the freekeh stir-fry between bowls, top with the egg and scatter over the remaining coriander and extra spring onions. Drizzle over the sriracha, if using, then serve with the lime wedges on the side.

Cook's tip

To bulk this out or for added protein, you could add 4 x 120g cooked and shredded skinless chicken breast fillets.

 11   7   2

 9   7   2   **SmartPoints value per serving**

Kimchi soba with prawns & edamame

serves 4   **prep time 15 minutes**   **cook time 10 minutes**

Spicy, tangy kimchi gives this simple dish added crunch and a real flavour boost, while the soba noodles add an even more authentic taste.

120g soba noodles

150g frozen edamame beans

1 red pepper, deseeded and thinly sliced

1 orange or yellow pepper, deseeded and thinly sliced

125g kimchi, thinly sliced, plus 2 tablespoons liquid from the jar

1 teaspoon toasted sesame oil

460g raw peeled king prawns, deveined

½ teaspoon Chinese five spice

Calorie controlled cooking spray

1   Cook the noodles in a pan of boiling water to pack instructions. Drain, then rinse and drain again. Meanwhile, in a separate pan, cook the edamame for 4-5 minutes until tender.

2   Transfer the noodles and edamame to a large bowl, add the pepper, kimchi and sesame oil, then season to taste and toss to combine.

3   Pat the prawns dry with kitchen paper then put in a small bowl with the Chinese five spice. Season and toss to coat. Mist a large nonstick frying pan with cooking spray and fry the prawns over a medium-high heat for 1-2 minutes on each side, until cooked through.

4   Divide the noodle mixture between bowls, top with the prawns and serve.

Cook's tip
Fancy more veggies? Cook some sugar snap peas in the same pan as the edamame and toss through the noodles. The SmartPoints will stay the same.

 SmartPoints value per serving

Steak au poivre

serves 4   **prep time 15 minutes**   **cook time 15 minutes**

Pepper-crusted sirloin steak is served with a shallot, courgette and brandy sauce in this showstopping recipe that's ideal for a special occasion.

1 tablespoon whole black peppercorns, crushed using a pestle and mortar

4 x 225g sirloin steaks, fat trimmed

2 teaspoons olive oil

1 large courgette, halved lengthwise and thinly sliced

3 shallots, finely chopped

3 tablespoons brandy or bourbon

250ml beef stock, made with ½ stock cube

1 tablespoon Dijon mustard

320g Tenderstem broccoli, to serve

1   Spread the crushed peppercorns onto a plate. Coat the steaks on one side with the peppercorns, pressing so they adhere, then season with salt.

2   Heat the oil in a large heavy nonstick frying pan over a medium-high heat. Add the steaks, peppercorn-side down, and cook for 2-3 minutes on each side, or until cooked to your liking. Transfer to a plate, cover loosely with kitchen foil and set aside to rest.

3   Add the courgette and shallots to the pan, season with a little salt and cook, stirring, for 3 minutes. Add the brandy and cook for 20 seconds (if the brandy flames, cover the frying pan with a lid and remove from the heat until it dies down). Whisk the stock and mustard into the pan until smooth, then simmer for 5 minutes, until the sauce is slightly thickened.

4   Meanwhile, cook the broccoli in a pan of boiling water for 4-5 minutes until tender, then drain and serve with the pepper steaks and courgette sauce.

Cook's tips

You can use any beef steak you like in this recipe – just remember to adjust the SmartPoints accordingly. If you'd rather not use alcohol in the sauce, you can substitute with the same quantity of stock.

7 **7** **7**   SmartPoints value per serving

Sri Lankan-style kotu roti

serves 2   prep time 20 minutes   cook time 25 minutes

Kotu roti is a popular street food all over Sri Lanka that mixes pieces of flatbread with vegetables, spices, chicken and eggs. Use a hot curry powder if you like it extra-spicy.

2 teaspoons vegetable oil

3 garlic cloves, crushed

20g fresh ginger, peeled and grated (or use 4 teaspoons ginger paste)

1 onion, diced

1 large tomato, diced

1 tablespoon mild curry powder

1 teaspoon ground cumin

1 tablespoon soy sauce

12 curry leaves

2 large carrots, cut into matchsticks

2 leeks, trimmed, halved, and finely sliced

250g white cabbage, roughly chopped

1 WW Wrap, cut into 2cm pieces

200g cooked skinless chicken breast fillets, shredded

1 large egg, beaten

4 tablespoons chopped fresh coriander

Lemon wedges, to serve

1 Put the oil in a large nonstick wok or frying pan with 250ml water and set over a medium-high heat. Add the garlic, ginger, onion and tomato and cook for 5 minutes until the onions are soft and the mixture becomes sauce-like.

2 Add the curry powder, cumin, soy sauce and curry leaves, and fry for another 2 minutes.

3 Add the carrots, leeks and cabbage, stir-frying for 10 minutes until the veg is almost tender – if it starts to stick or look dry, add a splash of water to the wok.

4 Add the WW Wrap, chicken and the beaten egg and cook for 5 minutes, or until the egg sets around the veg and the wrap softens a little. Stir through the coriander and season to taste, then serve with the lemon wedges.

7 **4** **4** SmartPoints value per serving

Cook's tip
Add extra protein with a second egg.

8 **4** **4**

Lemony pork piccata

serves 4   **prep time 20 minutes**   **cook time 10 minutes**

Piccata is an Italian dish in which the meat is sautéed with lemon, butter and capers. Chicken or veal is often used, but this version uses lean pork steaks.

4 x 120g lean pork loin steaks, fat trimmed

2 tablespoons plain flour

3 teaspoons butter

1 teaspoon olive oil

1 shallot, finely chopped

1 small garlic clove, crushed

120ml chicken stock, made with ½ stock cube

Zest and juice of 1 lemon

1 tablespoon drained capers

320g fine green beans, trimmed

2 tablespoons chopped fresh flat-leaf parsley

10g Parmesan, finely grated

1 Put the pork between two pieces of clingfilm, then flatten with a rolling pin to a 5mm thickness.

2 Put the flour in a shallow bowl, then season well. Coat the pork in the flour, shaking off any excess, then set aside on a plate.

3 Melt two-thirds of the butter in a large nonstick frying pan over a high heat and add the olive oil. Sear the pork for 2 minutes on each side – you may need to do this in batches – then remove from the pan and set aside. Cover loosely with kitchen foil to keep warm.

4 Add the shallot, garlic, stock, lemon juice and capers to the frying pan, then bring to the boil, scraping up any browned bits from the bottom of the pan. Reduce the heat to medium and cook, stirring occasionally, for 2 minutes until the sauce is slightly reduced. Stir in the remaining butter and season to taste. Return the pork and any resting juices to the pan, and turn to coat in the sauce.

5 Meanwhile, cook the green beans in a pan of boiling water for 2-3 minutes until just tender, then drain. In a small bowl, combine the parsley, Parmesan and lemon zest.

6 Divide the beans and pork between plates. Spoon the sauce over the pork then serve with the parsley mixture scattered over the top.

8 8 8   **SmartPoints value per serving**

Sweet potato lasagne with turkey & sage

serves 8   freezable   prep time 30 minutes + standing   cook time 1 hour 40 minutes

Our no-pasta lasagne layers thin slices of sweet potato with spinach, ricotta and a tasty turkey ragù, all topped with melting mozzarella.

2 teaspoons olive oil

1 large onion, diced

2 carrots, diced

3 garlic cloves, finely chopped

2 tablespoons chopped fresh sage

500g turkey breast mince

1½ tablespoons tomato purée

60ml red wine

400g tin chopped tomatoes

100g ricotta

1 large egg, beaten

200g young leaf spinach

2 sweet potatoes, peeled (total weight around 340g), and cut into 2.5mm-thick slices

100g light mozzarella, roughly torn

Cook's tip

Add a bit of heat to the mince mixture by adding 1 teaspoon chilli flakes to the pan at the same time as the tomatoes in Step 1.

1 Heat the oil in a nonstick pan over a medium-high heat and fry the onion and carrots for 5-6 minutes, until softened. Add the garlic and half the sage and cook for 1 minute. Stir in the turkey and tomato purée and cook for 5 minutes. Add the wine, simmer for 1-2 minutes, then stir in the tomatoes and 3 tablespoons water. Season then reduce the heat and simmer, covered, for 15 minutes, adding a splash of water if the mixture gets too thick.

2 In a bowl, combine the ricotta, egg and remaining sage, then season. Put the spinach in a large heatproof bowl and pour over boiling water from the kettle. Let stand for 1 minute, then drain and set aside to cool. Squeeze out any excess liquid, then chop.

3 Preheat the oven to 200°C, fan 180°C, gas mark 6. Assemble the lasagne: spread a thin layer of the turkey sauce over the base of a 25cm square baking dish. Cover with one-third of the sweet potato slices, making sure they overlap a little. Spread half the remaining turkey sauce over the potatoes, then cover with another third of sweet potatoes. Top with the spinach, then spoon the ricotta mixture over the top. Top with the remaining potato slices, remaining sauce and the mozzarella. Cover loosely with kitchen foil then transfer to a baking sheet.

4 Bake for 1 hour, until the sweet potatoes are tender, then remove the foil and bake for a further 10 minutes until the cheese is browned. Let stand for 10 minutes before serving.

The lasagne can be frozen in an airtight container for up to 3 months.

5   4   2   SmartPoints value per serving

Lamb curry with raita

serves 4   freezable   prep time 20 minutes   cook time 2 hours 15 minutes

This melt-in-the-mouth lamb curry is aromatic and rich, thanks to the addition of coconut milk and a few hours on the hob. It's a great recipe to batch cook and freeze.

2 teaspoons curry powder

¾ teaspoon ground cumin

½ teaspoon ground cinnamon

1½ tablespoons vegetable oil

450g lean lamb leg, trimmed of fat and diced

1 red onion, coarsely chopped

1 tablespoon grated fresh ginger

3 garlic cloves, finely chopped

Handful fresh coriander, leaves and stems roughly chopped

400g tin chopped tomatoes

125ml reduced-fat coconut milk

320g prepared butternut squash, diced

2 x 300g packs prepared cauliflower rice

FOR THE RAITA

120g fat-free natural yogurt

2 tablespoons chopped fresh coriander

½ teaspoon grated fresh ginger

¼ teaspoon ground cumin

1 In a small bowl, combine the curry powder, cumin and cinnamon, then season and set aside. Heat ½ tablespoon of the oil in a large casserole or nonstick pan set over a medium-high heat. Season the lamb with a little of the spice mixture then cook, in batches, for 2-3 minutes until browned all over. Transfer the lamb to a plate, using a slotted spoon, and set aside.

2 Heat ½ tablespoon of the remaining oil in the casserole, and fry the onion, ginger, garlic, coriander stems and remaining spice mixture for 4-5 minutes until softened. Return the lamb to the casserole, then add the tomatoes, coconut milk and half a tin of cold water. Bring to the boil, then reduce the heat and simmer gently, uncovered, for 1 hour, adding a little more water if the mixture gets too thick.

3 Add the butternut squash and cook for a further 1 hour, until the lamb is very tender, then stir in most of the coriander leaves.

4 Meanwhile, make the raita. Stir all the ingredients together in a small bowl until well combined.

5 Just before the curry is ready, prepare the cauliflower rice. Heat the remaining oil in a large nonstick frying pan set over a medium-high heat. Add the cauliflower rice and cook, stirring, for 2-3 minutes until cooked through. Season to taste.

6 Divide the cauliflower rice between bowls, spoon over the curry, scatter over the remaining coriander leaves and serve with the raita spooned over.

The curry (minus the raita and cauliflower rice) can be frozen in an airtight container for up to 3 months.

 9 8 8 SmartPoints value per serving

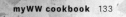

Beef & pinto bean chilli

serves 4   **freezable**   **prep time 10 minutes**   **cook time 30 minutes**

Chilli doesn't get any quicker or easier than this recipe that's cooked in 30 minutes. You can use whatever tinned beans you like – just remember to adjust the SmartPoints.

2 tablespoons vegetable oil

300g frozen sliced mixed peppers

100g frozen diced onion

1 large garlic clove, crushed

450g extra-lean 5% fat beef mince

400g tin pinto beans, drained and rinsed

2 x 400g tins chopped tomatoes

1½ teaspoons chipotle paste

2 teaspoons chilli powder

¼ teaspoon dried oregano

4 tablespoons reduced-fat soured cream, to serve

Handful fresh coriander leaves, to serve

1   Heat the oil in a large nonstick pan over a medium-high heat. Add the frozen vegetables and garlic and cook, stirring, for 5 minutes, or until the vegetables are thawed and any liquid has evaporated.

2   Increase the heat to high, add the beef to the pan and cook for 2 minutes, breaking up any lumps with a wooden spoon. Add the beans, tomatoes, chipotle paste, chilli powder and oregano, then season well and bring to a boil. Reduce the heat and simmer for 15 minutes until the beef is cooked through and the chilli has thickened.

3   Ladle the chilli into bowls, top with the soured cream and coriander, then serve.

The chilli can be frozen in an airtight container for up to 3 months.

10 **6** **6**   **SmartPoints value per serving**

Cook's tip

If you like, serve the chilli with 4 x 40g corn tortillas, warmed to pack instructions. The recipe will no longer be gluten free.

14 **10** **10**

Chicken & aubergine in black bean sauce

serves 4   prep time 15 minutes   cook time 25 minutes

Tender chicken and aubergines are stir-fried with black bean sauce and served with rice noodles in this easy dish that's packed with Asian flavours.

200g rice noodles

2 teaspoons vegetable oil

600g skinless chicken breast fillets, cut into bite-size pieces

350g baby aubergines, trimmed and quartered (see Cook's tip)

4 garlic cloves, thinly sliced

2 teaspoons grated fresh ginger

½ teaspoon chilli flakes

180ml chicken stock, made with 1 stock cube

½ x 120g sachet black bean stir-fry sauce (we used Sainsbury's)

1 red pepper, deseeded and cut into bite-size pieces

5 spring onions, trimmed and cut into 2.5cm pieces

2 tablespoons light soy sauce

1 tablespoon rice wine vinegar

1 tablespoon cornflour

1 tablespoon sesame seeds

1 Cook the rice noodles to pack instructions, then drain well and set aside.

2 Meanwhile, heat half the oil in a large nonstick wok or frying pan set over a high heat. Add half the chicken and stir-fry for 3-5 minutes, until browned all over. Transfer to a large bowl, then repeat with the remaining oil and chicken.

3 Add the aubergine to the wok and stir-fry for 3 minutes, adding a splash of water if it starts to stick, then add the garlic, ginger and chilli flakes and stir-fry for a further 1 minute. In a small bowl, combine the stock and black bean sauce, then add the mixture to the wok. Stir-fry for 5 minutes, until the aubergine is tender, then add the pepper and spring onions and toss to combine. Return the chicken to the wok and stir-fry for 1-2 minutes.

4 In a small bowl, whisk together the soy sauce, vinegar and cornflour, then add the mixture to the work and stir-fry for 2 minutes until the sauce has thickened and the chicken is cooked through.

5 Divide the noodles between bowls, top with the stir-fry and serve garnished with the sesame seeds.

Cook's tip
If you can't find baby aubergines, just use regular ones, cut into large chunks.

 9 8 8   SmartPoints value per serving

Tex-Mex turkey steaks with sweetcorn salad

serves 4   prep time 15 minutes   cook time 10 minutes

Turkey steaks are a great alternative to chicken breast fillets. Here, they're griddled with some cayenne pepper, to give them a little kick

Calorie controlled cooking spray

4 x 125g turkey breast steaks

Pinch of cayenne pepper

FOR THE SWEETCORN SALAD

400g frozen corn kernels

1 green chilli, deseeded and diced

1 tomato, diced

2 spring onions, trimmed and thinly sliced

1 green pepper, deseeded and finely chopped

2 tablespoons chopped fresh coriander

Juice of 1 lime (you'll need 2 tablespoons, plus wedges to serve

2 teaspoons extra-virgin olive oil

1   Make the sweetcorn salad. Cook the sweetcorn in a pan of boiling water for 4-5 minutes until tender, then drain and transfer to a serving bowl. Let cool, then add the remaining salad ingredients to the bowl, season to taste and toss to combine. Set aside.

2   Mist a large nonstick griddle pan with cooking spray and set over a medium-high heat. Season the turkey breast steaks, then sprinkle over the cayenne pepper. Griddle the turkey steaks for 3 minutes on each side, until cooked through and golden.

3   Serve the turkey with the sweetcorn salad and lime wedges for squeezing over.

6   1   1   SmartPoints value per serving

Korean chicken drumsticks

serves 4   prep time 15 minutes   cook time 45 minutes

Chicken drumsticks are packed with flavour and make a nice change from breast fillet. These are coated in a sticky, spicy glaze, then baked and served with rice and veg.

8 chicken drumsticks, skin removed

2 tablespoons light soy sauce

1 tablespoon rice wine vinegar

1 teaspoon toasted sesame oil

3 garlic cloves, crushed

2 teaspoons grated fresh ginger

1 teaspoon sriracha sauce

2 teaspoons light brown soft sugar

240g basmati rice

2 pak choi, trimmed and quartered lengthwise

2 teaspoons sesame seeds

1 Preheat the oven to 190°C, fan 170°C, gas mark 5. Line a small baking tray with kitchen foil.

2 Cut shallow slits into the drumsticks, then put on the prepared baking tray. Combine the soy sauce, vinegar, oil, garlic, ginger, sriracha and sugar in a small bowl, then pour half the sauce over the chicken. Turn to coat then bake for 20 minutes. Turn the chicken and spoon over the remaining sauce. Bake for a further 20 minutes, until the chicken is tender and cooked through and the sauce is slightly sticky. Transfer the chicken to a plate, then cover with kitchen foil and set aside.

3 Pour the pan juices into a small pan and simmer over a medium-low heat for 4 minutes until slightly thickened.

4 Meanwhile, cook the rice to pack instructions until tender, and steam the pak choi over a pan of boiling water for 4-5 minutes.

5 Divide the rice between plates and top with the chicken and pak choi. Drizzle over the reduced pan juices and scatter over the sesame seeds to serve.

Cook's tip
If you prefer, you can use brown basmati rice instead of white.

(10) (10) (10) **SmartPoints value per serving**

Griddled sea bass with lemons & tomato vinaigrette

serves 4   prep time 15 minutes   cook time 10 minutes

When you want a super-quick dinner on the table, griddled fish is a great option. This dish of sea bass with a simple sauce of fresh tomatoes is ready in less than half an hour.

Calorie controlled cooking spray

2 lemons, halved

4 x 120g sea bass fillets

2 teaspoons extra-virgin olive oil

400g bunch asparagus, trimmed

FOR THE TOMATO VINAIGRETTE

250g cherry tomatoes, diced

1 shallot, finely diced

1 teaspoon drained capers, chopped

½ small garlic clove, finely chopped

1 tablespoon lemon juice

2 teaspoons extra-virgin olive oil

1 tablespoons chopped fresh chives

2 teaspoons chopped fresh flat-leaf parsley

1   To make the vinaigrette, combine the tomatoes, shallot, capers, garlic, lemon juice and oil in a small pan. Season and cook over a medium heat for 3 minutes, stirring occasionally, until warm. Remove from the heat and stir in the herbs.

2   Meanwhile, mist a large nonstick griddle or frying pan with cooking spray and set over a medium-high heat. Brush the cut sides of the lemon and the sea bass fillets with the oil then season the fish. Griddle the lemons, cut-side down for 3-4 minutes until charred, then remove from the pan. Griddle the fish, skin-side down, for 2-3 minutes until the skin is crisp, then turn over and cook for a further 2 minutes. Remove from the pan.

3   Meanwhile, blanch the asparagus in a pan of boiling water for 2-3 minutes until just tender. Drain.

4   Divide the fish, asparagus and lemons between plates. Spoon the tomato vinaigrette over the fish and serve.

 **3** **2** **2**   SmartPoints value per serving

Cook's tip
Try serving this with 700g boiled and crushed new potatoes.

 6 **5** **2**

Jackfruit tacos with sriracha mayonnaise

serves 4   prep time 20 minutes   cook time 35 minutes

You can find young jackfruit in most supermarkets nowadays – it has a meaty texture, so is ideal for creating vegan recipes, like these colourful tacos.

2 x 410g tins young jackfruit in water, drained

3 teaspoons vegetable oil

½ onion, finely diced

2 garlic cloves, finely chopped

2 teaspoons chilli powder

½ teaspoon dried oregano

1 teaspoon ground cumin

1 ½ tablespoons tomato purée

400g tin black beans, drained and rinsed

½ teaspoon chipotle paste

8 x 20g small white corn tortillas (we used Old El Paso)

1 avocado, peeled, stone removed, and thinly sliced

80g shredded red cabbage

Handful fresh coriander leaves, to serve

FOR THE SRIRACHA MAYONNAISE

40g vegan mayonnaise (we used Hellmann's)

2 teaspoons lime juice

¾ teaspoon sriracha sauce

1 Thinly slice the jackfruit, then shred it using your fingers and set aside.

2 Heat 2 teaspoons of the oil in large nonstick frying pan set over a medium heat. Add the onion and garlic and cook, stirring often, for 5 minutes, until softened. Stir in the chilli powder, oregano, half the cumin, and a pinch of salt, then cook for 1 minute, until fragrant. Stir in the jackfruit, tomato purée and 125ml water. Bring the mixture to the boil, then reduce the heat and cook, covered, for 25 minutes until the jackfruit is very tender, adding more water if the mixture starts to stick to the pan.

3 Meanwhile, put the black beans and chipotle paste in a small microwave-safe bowl along with the remaining oil, cumin and a pinch of salt. Cover with kitchen paper and microwave on High for 1-2 minutes, stirring every 30 seconds, until very hot. Remove from the microwave and set aside to keep warm.

4 To make the sriracha mayonnaise, combine all the ingredients in a small bowl. Warm the tortillas in the microwave for 10 seconds then fill with the jackfruit mixture, chipotle beans, avocado and cabbage. Drizzle over the sriracha mayonnaise and serve two tacos per serving, garnished with the coriander.

 SmartPoints value per serving

Weekday spaghetti

serves 4   prep time 10 minutes   cook time 15 minutes

Broccoli is the star of the show in this easy Italian-inspired pasta dish. The chilli flakes bring some welcome heat, but you can use red pepper flakes for a milder, sweeter result.

180g wholewheat spaghetti

300g Tenderstem broccoli, trimmed

1 tablespoon olive oil

3 garlic cloves, thinly sliced

½ teaspoon chilli flakes, plus extra to garnish

6 anchovy fillets, drained and finely chopped

20g Parmesan, shaved, to serve

1 Cook the pasta in a large pan of boiling water to pack instructions until al dente, adding the broccoli to the pan for the last 2 minutes of cooking time. Drain, reserving 60ml of the pasta cooking water.

2 Meanwhile, heat the oil in large, deep nonstick sauté pan set over medium heat. Add the garlic and chilli flakes, then cook, stirring constantly, for 1 minute. Add the anchovies and cook for 1 minute, stirring frequently, until the anchovies soften.

3 Add the pasta and broccoli to the pan, season well and toss together. Cook for 1-2 minutes, adding the reserved cooking liquid if the mixture seems a little dry.

4 Divide the pasta between plates, then scatter over the shaved Parmesan and extra chilli flakes to serve.

Cook's tip
The anchovies add a salty richness but if you're not keen on them, simply leave them out.

6 **6** **2**

7 **7** **2**   SmartPoints value per serving

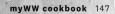

Jerk chicken with quinoa, mint & mango salad

serves 4   prep time 15 minutes   cook time 25 minutes

The fresh, sweet peppers and mango in the colourful salad go perfectly with spicy chicken in this easy but impressive dish.

200g tricolour quinoa, rinsed well

4 x 165g skinless chicken breast fillets

1 tablespoon jerk seasoning

Calorie controlled cooking spray

1 large mango, peeled, stone removed, and diced

1 red pepper, deseeded and diced

Large handful mint, leaves picked and chopped

Large handful coriander, leaves picked and chopped, plus extra leaves to serve

2 spring onions, trimmed and thinly sliced

Lime wedges, to serve

FOR THE SALAD DRESSING

Grated zest and juice of 2 limes

4 teaspoons olive oil

¼ small red onion, very finely diced

1   Toast the quinoa in a small pan set over a medium heat for 5 minutes, stirring constantly, until dry and fragrant. Stir in 375ml water and season well. Bring to the boil over a high heat, then reduce the heat to low and simmer, covered, for 15 minutes, until the liquid is absorbed and the quinoa is tender. Remove from the heat and let stand for 5 minutes before fluffing up the quinoa with a fork. Transfer to a large bowl and let cool slightly.

2   Meanwhile, put the chicken between two pieces of clingfilm and use a rolling pin to flatten to a thickness of approximately 1cm. Rub the jerk seasoning into the chicken then season well and mist all over with cooking spray. Mist a large nonstick griddle pan with cooking spray and set over a medium-high heat. Griddle the chicken for 5 minutes on each side, then transfer to a plate and let rest for 5 minutes – you may need to do this in batches.

3   To make the salad dressing, whisk together the lime juice and olive oil, then season to taste and stir in the zest and onion.

4   Add the mango, pepper, herbs and spring onions to the quinoa. Drizzle over the dressing and toss to combine. Divide between plates, scatter over the extra coriander and serve with the chicken and lime wedges on the side.

Cook's tip
If you can't find tricolour quinoa, just use the regular version instead.

8 7 2

9 7 2 **SmartPoints value per serving**

Stuffed pasta shells

serves 6   prep time 20 minutes   cook time 30 minutes

Filling jumbo pasta shells with a ricotta and herb stuffing makes this vegetarian recipe just that little bit different. You could use cannelloni if you can't find the shells.

180g jumbo pasta shells, also known as conchiglioni rigati (you'll need 24 shells)

Calorie controlled cooking spray

280g ricotta

300g fat-free cottage cheese

1 egg, lightly beaten

1 garlic clove, crushed

2 tablespoons chopped fresh flat-leaf parsley

1 teaspoon dried oregano

½ quantity (you'll need about 500g) Tomato sauce (see recipe, p34)

20g vegetarian Italian-style hard cheese, grated

1 Cook the shells in a very large pan of boiling water for 10 minutes, or until al dente. Drain well and set aside to cool slightly.

2 Preheat the oven to 190°C, fan 170°C, gas mark 5. Mist a large rectangular baking dish with cooking spray.

3 Meanwhile, combine the ricotta, cottage cheese, egg, garlic, parsley and oregano in a bowl, then season and set aside.

4 Spread one third of the tomato sauce over the base of the prepared baking dish, then arrange the shells on top. Fill each shell with the ricotta mixture, then spoon over the remaining sauce. Scatter over the grated cheese and bake for 20 minutes, or until the sauce is bubbling and the cheese has melted.

6 6 5   SmartPoints value per serving

Cook's tip
For extra flavour, cut 8 drained anchovies into thirds, and arrange one piece on the top of each shell before spooning over the sauce – the SmartPoints will remain the same.

Courgette, lemon & feta risotto

serves 4   freezable   prep time 20 minutes   cook time 30 minutes (◑) (◑) (◑)

Risotto is a simple yet impressive dish to make. This one is packed with plenty of fresh warm-weather veggies and herbs, zesty lemon and salty feta.

Calorie controlled cooking spray

4 large courgettes; 3 diced, the other grated

1 onion, finely diced

2 garlic cloves, crushed

1.5 litres vegetable stock, made with 1 stock cube

250g Arborio rice

2 spring onions, trimmed and finely sliced

Grated zest and juice of 1 lemon

20g vegetarian Italian-style hard cheese, finely grated

20 basil leaves, shredded

40g light feta

100g watercress, to serve

1 Preheat the oven to 200°C, fan 180°C, gas mark 6. Mist a large baking tray with cooking spray. Scatter the diced courgette over the baking tray, mist with more cooking spray, then season and roast for 20-25 minutes until soft and golden.

2 Meanwhile, mist a large, nonstick frying pan with cooking spray and fry the onion over a low heat for 10 minutes until soft, then add the garlic and cook for another 2 minutes.

3 While the onion is cooking, bring the stock to a simmer in a medium pan, then reduce the heat to low.

4 Add the rice to the frying pan, increase the heat to medium-high and cook, stirring constantly, for 2 minutes. Add the stock, a ladleful at a time, only adding more after the rice has absorbed the liquid. After 15 minutes, add the grated courgette, then continue adding the stock until it is all used up, and the rice is creamy and tender.

5 Remove the risotto from the heat and stir in the roasted courgettes, spring onions, lemon zest and juice, grated cheese and shredded basil. Season to taste, then cover with a lid and let stand for 2 minutes.

6 Divide the risotto between bowls and serve topped with the feta and watercress.

The risotto (minus the feta and watercress garnish) can be frozen in an airtight container for up to 3 months.

Cook's tip
You could use the homemade Vegetable stock (see recipe, p36) in place of the stock cube in this recipe.

(8) (8) (8) **SmartPoints value per serving**

Bangers, baked beans & butternut squash bake

serves 4   freezable   prep time 20 minutes   cook time 1 hour 5 minutes

This makes a hearty all-in-one dinner on a chilly evening. It freezes well, so why not make it ahead of time and reheat it when you want something on the table quickly.

1 butternut squash

Calorie controlled cooking spray

1 batch Soffrito (see recipe, p34), defrosted if frozen

1 yellow pepper, deseeded and diced

680g passata

1 tablespoon red wine vinegar

2 teaspoons sweet smoked paprika

2 teaspoons dried oregano, plus an extra pinch

1 teaspoon ground cumin

2 tablespoons brown sauce

6 reduced-fat pork sausages

2 x 400g tins borlotti beans

1 Peel the squash, then cut in half to separate the rounded, seeded end from the straight trunk. Halve and de-seed the rounded end, then dice. Slice the trunk into 5mm-thick rounds.

2 Mist a large flameproof casserole with cooking spray and cook the soffrito, pepper and diced squash over a medium heat for 3 minutes, until the pepper starts to soften. Add the passata, red wine vinegar, paprika, oregano, cumin and brown sauce, then season. Stir in 350ml water, then bring to the boil. Reduce the heat and simmer, covered, for 15 minutes.

3 Mist a nonstick frying pan with cooking spray and brown the sausages over a medium heat for 2-3 minutes. Remove from the heat, cut in half and add to the casserole along with the beans. Bring to a simmer and cook, uncovered, for 5 minutes, until thickened.

4 Preheat the oven to 200°C, fan 180°C, gas mark 6. Arrange the squash rounds over the top of the casserole, mist with cooking spray and scatter over the extra oregano. Season then transfer the casserole to the oven and bake for 30-35 minutes until the squash topping is tender and golden.

The casserole can be frozen in an airtight container for up to 3 months.

Cook's tip
Try serving this with steamed broccoli for no extra SmartPoints.

6 4 4 SmartPoints value per serving

Tagliatelle tuna puttanesca

serves 4   freezable   prep time 10 minutes   cook time 30 minutes

Puttanesca is a popular pasta dish that usually calls for anchovies, but this version uses tinned tuna instead. Make it quick by using our make-ahead soffrito and tomato sauce.

1 teaspoon olive oil

2 garlic cloves, finely sliced

1 batch Soffrito (see recipe, p34), defrosted if frozen

1 quantity Tomato sauce (see recipe, p34), defrosted if frozen

1 teaspoon balsamic vinegar

1 teaspoon agave syrup

¼ teaspoon chilli flakes

1 tablespoon drained capers, plus an extra 2 teaspoons to serve

240g wholewheat tagliatelle

Small handful fresh flat-leaf parsley, chopped, plus extra leaves to serve

Juice of ½ lemon

2 x 140g tins tuna in spring water, drained and flaked

1 Heat the oil in a large nonstick pan set over a medium heat, then fry the garlic for 2 minutes, until golden. Stir in the soffrito, tomato sauce, vinegar, agave syrup, chilli flakes, capers and 250ml water. Bring to the boil, then reduce the heat and simmer for 20 minutes until thickened.

2 Meanwhile, bring a large pan of water to the boil and cook the tagliatelle to pack instructions until al dente. Drain.

3 Stir most of the parsley and all of the lemon juice and tuna into the sauce, then season to taste. Cook for a further 2-3 minutes, until warmed through.

4 Toss the pasta and sauce together, then serve with the extra capers and parsley scattered over the top.

8   8   2 SmartPoints value per serving

Cook's tip
Puttanesca traditionally contains lots of olives – add 25g thinly sliced black olives, if you like.

Smoky bean & barley burgers

makes 6   freezable   prep time 25 minutes   cook time 55 minutes

These grain-based burgers tick all the boxes for hearty flavour and texture. You can make the burger patties ahead of time, freeze, then defrost when you want to serve them.

100g pearl barley, rinsed

Calorie controlled cooking spray

1 green chilli, finely chopped

1 onion, finely chopped

198g tin sweetcorn, drained

2 garlic cloves, crushed

1 teaspoon smoked paprika

¼ teaspoon cayenne pepper

400g tin pinto beans in water, drained and rinsed

Handful fresh coriander, chopped

1 egg, lightly beaten

20g vegetarian Italian hard-style cheese, grated

2 teaspoons vegetable oil

4 tablespoons 0% fat natural Greek yogurt

Juice of ½ lime

6 x 60g wholemeal burger buns

1 Baby Gem lettuce, leaves separated

1   Bring a pan of water to the boil, add the barley then bring back to the boil. Reduce the heat and simmer for 35 minutes, or until tender. Drain well and spread out on a large plate to cool.

2   Meanwhile, mist a large nonstick frying pan with cooking spray and set over a medium heat. Cook the chilli, onion and sweetcorn, stirring occasionally, for 10 minutes or until the vegetables start to brown. Add the garlic, paprika and cayenne pepper and cook, stirring, for 30 seconds. Transfer to a plate to cool and wipe the pan clean with kitchen paper.

3   Put the beans in a food processor and pulse until coarsely chopped. Transfer to a large bowl, add the cooled barley along with the chilli and onion mixture, coriander, egg and cheese. Season and stir to combine. Transfer half of the mixture to a food processor and process until finely chopped but not completely smooth. Return the mixture to the bowl and stir to combine. Divide the bean mixture into 6 equal balls, then flatten to form 10cm round patties.

4   Add the oil to the frying pan and set over a medium heat. Cook the burgers, in batches, for 5 minutes on each side, until cooked through.

5   Meanwhile, combine the yogurt and lime juice and season.

6   Split the burger buns and toast until golden, then top with the lettuce, bean burgers, lime yogurt and bun tops.

The burger patties can be frozen in a freezer bag, separated by small pieces of baking paper, for up to 3 months.

 SmartPoints value per burger

10   7   7

Turkey shepherd's pie

serves 8   prep time 20 minutes   cook time 1 hour

A much-loved family favourite, this would normally use lamb mince, but we've used turkey mince instead to keep the SmartPoints lower – it's just as delicious!

800g potatoes, peeled and chopped

100g reduced-fat soured cream

1 tablespoon low-fat spread

3 teaspoons olive oil

3 carrots, diced

2 celery sticks, diced

1 small onion, diced

160g frozen sweetcorn kernels

2 garlic cloves, finely chopped

500g turkey breast mince

1½ tablespoons tomato purée

½ teaspoon dried rosemary (or 1 sprig fresh, leaves stripped and finely chopped)

1 teaspoon dried thyme (or 2 fresh sprigs, leaved stripped and finely chopped)

2 tablespoons plain flour

300ml chicken stock, made with ½ stock cube

Calorie controlled cooking spray

Cook's tips

You can assemble the shepherd's pie up to 2 days ahead, cover it, and refrigerate it unbaked. Remove the covering before popping it into the oven; add an extra few minutes to the cooking time. Serve with steamed green veg on the side, for no extra SmartPoints.

1 Put the potatoes in a large pan, cover with cold water and bring to the boil over a high heat. Reduce the heat and simmer for 15 minutes, until just tender. Drain and return to the pan, then add the soured cream and low-fat spread. Season to taste and mash until smooth.

2 Meanwhile, heat 2 teaspoons of the oil in a large frying pan over a medium heat. Add the carrots, celery and onion and cook, stirring, for 6-8 minutes until softened. Stir in the corn and garlic and cook, stirring constantly, for 1 minute. Transfer to a bowl and set aside.

3 Heat the remaining oil in the pan and cook the turkey for 5 minutes, breaking up any lumps with a wooden spoon, until browned. Stir in the tomato purée, rosemary and thyme, then season and cook for 2 minutes. Return the carrot mixture to the pan, stir in the flour and chicken stock and cook for 2 minutes, stirring, until thickened.

4 Preheat the oven to 200°C, fan 180°C, gas mark 6, and mist a 20cm x 30cm baking dish with cooking spray.

5 Spoon the turkey mince mixture into the prepared baking dish then spread over the mashed potatoes. Bake for 35-40 minutes until the filling is bubbling and the potato topping is golden.

6 5 2   **SmartPoints value per serving**

Recipe builder
WW Wraps

How's this for a clever idea – turn a pack of WW Wraps into spicy tortilla chips to enjoy as a snack, or use them to add crunch and flavour to these other easy recipes.

Smoky spiced tortilla chips

serves 4
prep time 10 minutes
cook time 8 minutes

Preheat the oven to 200°C, fan 180°C, gas mark 6. In a small bowl, combine 1½ teaspoons **sweet paprika**, 1 teaspoon **dried oregano**, ¼ teaspoon **garlic salt** and a pinch of **cayenne pepper**, then season with **freshly ground black pepper**. Mist 4 **WW White Wraps** with **calorie controlled cooking spray** on one side, then scatter over half the spice mix. Turn the wraps over, mist with more cooking spray and scatter over the remaining spice mix. Using kitchen scissors, cut each wrap into crisp-size triangles. Arrange the triangles in a single layer on non-stick baking sheets and bake for 6-8 minutes until crisp and golden. Set aside to cool, then serve alongside spicy suppers like Beef & pinto chilli on p138 or in the recipes, right.

4 **4** **4**   SmartPoints value per serving

Feta & black bean nachos

serves 4
prep time 10 minutes
cook time 20 minutes

Make a batch of **Smoky spiced tortilla chips** (see recipe, left), then keep the oven at 200°C, fan 180°C, gas mark 6. On the same baking tray, layer the tortilla chips with 300g deseeded and sliced **yellow cherry tomatoes**, 3 trimmed and thinly sliced **spring onions**, 50g drained **sliced jalapeños in brine** and a drained and rinsed 400g tin of **black beans**. Crumble over 200g **light feta** and bake for 8-10 minutes until the feta is turning golden. Meanwhile, combine 200g **0% fat natural Greek yogurt** and a handful of chopped **coriander** leaves in a bowl, then season to taste. Serve the nachos with shredded **iceberg lettuce**, and the yogurt and coriander mixture on the side.

9 **7** **7**   SmartPoints value per serving

Spicy corn chowder

serves 4
prep time 10 minutes
cook time 25 minutes

Make a batch of **Smoky spiced tortilla chips** (see recipe, far left). Put 1 batch **Soffrito** (see recipe, p34), 2 x 400g tins **chopped tomatoes**, 2 teaspoons **mild chilli powder**, the juice of 2 **limes**, 2 teaspoons **cumin seeds** and 1 **vegetable stock cube** in a large pan with 400ml water. Cover and bring to the boil, then reduce the heat and simmer for 5 minutes. Add 400g frozen **sweetcorn**, a drained 400g tin **black beans**, 25g drained and chopped **sliced red jalapeños in brine** and a handful of chopped **fresh coriander**. Simmer for a further 2 minutes to heat through, then serve with the tortilla chips.

10 **5** **5** **SmartPoints value per serving**

Tuna & olive panzanella

serves 4
prep time 20 minutes

Make a batch of **Smoky spiced tortilla chips** (see recipe, far left). Store half in an airtight container for another day, then roughly break up the remainder and set aside. Chop 1kg mixed **tomatoes** into bite-size pieces, then put them into a large bowl. Pour over 1 quantity **Vinaigrette** made without the water (see recipe, p36). Season to taste and toss to combine. Add 1 small thinly sliced **red onion**, a handful of chopped **fresh flat-leaf parsley**, 20g thinly sliced **pitted black olives** and 4 teaspoons drained **capers**. Drain and flake 2 x 145g tins **tuna in spring water**, then add to the bowl and stir to combine. Fold through the tortilla chips just before serving.

4 **3** **3** **SmartPoints value per serving**

Desserts

Four variations
Frozen fruit

For quick and easy desserts, prepared frozen fruit is genius. Fill your freezer with a range of different varieties and you can enjoy a vast seasonal selection all year round.

Frozen summer fruits with mint sugar
serves 2
prep time 5 minutes

Scatter 200g **frozen summer fruits** over a dessert plate and set aside. In a mini food processor, blitz together 6 large **mint leaves** and 4 teaspoons **granulated sugar** until the mint is finely chopped. Scatter the mint sugar over the berries and serve.

3 **3** **3** SmartPoints value per serving

Tropical fruit & wine ice lollies
makes 4
prep time 10 minutes + freezing

Combine 100ml **dry white wine** and 150ml **low-calorie lemonade** in a small jug and set aside. Divide 100g **frozen tropical smoothie mix** equally between 4 x 80ml ice-lolly moulds. Pour the wine mixture over the fruit and insert wooden lolly sticks or cover with the lids. Freeze for 5-6 hours or overnight, until set. To serve, dip each mould in hot water for a few seconds to release the ice lollies.

1 **1** **1** SmartPoints value per ice lolly

Nectarine & banana ice 'cream'
serves 2
prep time 5 minutes + freezing

Put 100g **frozen nectarine or peach** slices and 75g **frozen banana** slices in a mini food processor, or the small bowl of a large processor. Add 85g **fat-free natural yogurt**, then process until the mixture is smooth, creamy and ice cream-like in texture – you'll need to scrape down the sides a couple of times. Serve with a few extra slices of chopped nectarine scattered over the top.

1 **0** **0** SmartPoints value per serving

Frozen red berries with white chocolate custard
serves 1
prep time 5 minutes
cook time 5 minutes

Combine ½ teaspoon **custard powder** and 3 tablespoons **skimmed milk** in a microwave-safe jug and microwave on Medium for 30 seconds, then stir and return to the microwave for another 30 seconds. Repeat until you have a thick but pourable custard mixture. Stir in 15g chopped **white chocolate** until melted. To serve, arrange 125g **frozen red berries** over a plate, then drizzle over the hot custard.

5 **5** **5** SmartPoints value per serving

Avocado chocolate cake

serves 16   **prep time 20 minutes + cooling**   **cook time 45 minutes**

Ready to venture beyond avo on toast? Turn your hand to this rich, dark, totally delicious cake that replaces butter with avocado.

Calorie controlled cooking spray

100g dark chocolate (50% cocoa solids), chopped

175g plain flour

50g unsweetened cocoa powder

150g caster sugar

1 teaspoon baking powder

¾ teaspoon bicarbonate of soda

200g fat-free natural yogurt

85g avocado flesh

2 eggs

2 teaspoons vanilla extract

1 teaspoon icing sugar, to decorate

Small handful fresh mint leaves (optional), to decorate

1   Preheat the oven to 180°C, fan 160°C, gas mark 4. Line the base of a 20cm round cake tin with baking paper, and mist the sides with cooking spray.

2   Melt the chocolate in a microwave-safe bowl in 20-second bursts, stirring after each burst. Set aside to cool slightly.

3   In a large bowl, stir together the flour, cocoa powder, caster sugar, baking powder, bicarbonate of soda and a pinch of salt.

4   Put the yogurt and avocado in a blender and blitz to a purée. Add the eggs and vanilla extract and blitz until combined.

5   Add the yogurt mixture and melted chocolate to the dry ingredients, along with 100ml boiling water and stir until smooth and combined. Pour into the prepared tin, level the surface with a spatula and bake for 40-45 minutes, or until a skewer inserted into the centre of the cake comes out clean.

6   Cool in the tin for 10 minutes, then turn the cake out onto a wire rack to cool completely. Dust the top of the cake with the icing sugar and decorate with the mint leaves, if using.

The cake can be stored in an airtight container for up to 5 days.

Cook's tip
Serve each slice of cake with 1 tablespoon 0% fat natural Greek yogurt, if you like.

 SmartPoints value per serving

Autumn fruits clafoutis

serves 6   prep time 10 minutes   cook time 30 minutes

Juicy pears and blackberries are baked in a custard-style batter, then served warm with a spoonful of yogurt. It's the perfect pud for a chilly evening.

50g plain flour

40g golden caster sugar

2 eggs, lightly beaten

250ml skimmed milk

½ teaspoon vanilla extract

25g low-fat spread, melted

Grated zest of ½ orange

Calorie controlled cooking spray

2 pears, peeled, cored and cut into thick wedges

150g blackberries

1 teaspoon icing sugar, for dusting

120g 0% fat natural Greek yogurt, to serve

1 Preheat the oven to 180°C, fan 160°C, gas mark 4.

2 Sift the flour into a large mixing bowl, add a pinch of salt then stir in the caster sugar. Make a well in the centre, add the eggs, milk, vanilla and melted spread, then whisk until you have a smooth batter. Stir in the orange zest.

3 Mist a 22cm square shallow baking dish with cooking spray. Pour the batter into the dish, then arrange the pears and blackberries over the top. Bake for 28-30 minutes, until just set but with a slight wobble in the centre.

4 Remove from the oven and set aside to cool slightly, then sift over the icing sugar. Cut into 6 portions and serve each with 1 tablespoon of the yogurt.

5 4 4   SmartPoints value per serving

Mini lime cheesecake tarts

makes 18   **prep time 15 minutes + chilling**   🥕

These mini dessert treats are filled with a zesty soft cheese and lime mixture, and use ready-made tart cases, which makes them super-quick to prepare.

110g medium-fat soft cheese

3 tablespoons 0% fat natural Greek yogurt

35g caster sugar

Finely grated zest of 2 limes and juice of 1 lime

1 teaspoon vanilla extract

18 mini tart cases (we used Sainsbury's Taste the Difference sweet all butter pastry cases)

12g toasted flaked almonds

1   Put the soft cheese and yogurt into a medium bowl and stir until smooth and combined, taking care not to overmix or it will become runny. Beat in the sugar, lime juice, vanilla and half the lime zest. Refrigerate for 1-2 hours to firm up.

2   Spoon the mixture into the mini tart cases, scatter over the remaining lime zest and top with the flaked almonds. Serve immediately.

2 2 2   SmartPoints value per tart

Cook's tip
You can make the filling up to 2 days ahead but it's best to fill the tart cases just before serving so they stay crisp.

Chocolate butternut brownies

makes 12   prep time 10 minutes + cooling   cook time 45 minutes

Thanks to the butternut squash purée, these fantastically fudgy brownies contain natural sugars and vitamins, and are low in fat. Genius!

Calorie controlled cooking spray

300g butternut squash flesh, cut into 2cm pieces

100g dark chocolate (50% cocoa solids), chopped

4 eggs

200g golden caster sugar

50g cocoa powder

75g plain flour

2 teaspoons baking powder

½ teaspoon icing sugar, for dusting

1   Preheat the oven to 180°C, fan 160°C, gas mark 4. Mist a 20cm square cake tin with cooking spray and line with baking paper.

2   Put the squash in a microwave-safe bowl, splash a little water over and cover with clingfilm. Microwave on High for 10-12 minutes until tender. Drain off any excess liquid, then stir in the chocolate – the heat from the squash will melt the chocolate. Using a hand-held blender, blitz the mixture to a rough purée, then set aside to cool.

3   Using a hand-held electric whisk, beat together the eggs and caster sugar in a large bowl until the mixture is pale and fluffy. Fold through the cocoa powder, flour, baking powder and a pinch of salt.

4   Fold in the squash mixture, then pour into the prepared tin. Bake for 25-30 minutes until the brownies have set. Remove from the oven and let cool in the tin for at least 1 hour. Cut into 12 brownies, dust with icing sugar and serve.

Cook's tip
Serve each brownie with 1 tablespoon 0% fat natural Greek yogurt, if you like. The SmartPoints will be the same.

 **SmartPoints value per brownie**

Coconut-chocolate ice-cream bonbons

makes 24   freezable   prep time 30 minutes + freezing (v) (w) (%)

Toasted coconut brings a whole new flavour dimension to ice cream – these mini scoops are just the right size for an after-dinner treat.

100g desiccated or shredded coconut

500ml reduced-fat vanilla ice cream

80g dark chocolate (54% cocoa solids), chopped

1 Line a small baking sheet with baking paper and put in the freezer 1 hour before making the bonbons.

2 Preheat the oven to 160°C, fan 140°C, gas mark 3. Put the coconut on a foil-lined baking sheet and bake for 4-6 minutes or until golden, then remove from the oven and set aside to cool completely.

3 Make the bonbons one at a time. Using a mini ice-cream scoop, melon baller or tablespoon, scoop the ice cream into small balls (each weighing 20g), then quickly roll in the coconut. Transfer to the baking sheet in the freezer and repeat until you have 24 bonbons. Freeze for at least 6 hours or overnight (if freezing overnight, cover the bonbons with kitchen foil).

4 Up to four hours before serving, melt the chocolate in a microwave-safe bowl in 20-second intervals, stirring after each interval. Let cool slightly.

5 Remove the bonbons from the freezer, drizzle over the melted chocolate, then return to the freezer to set. Arrange on a platter to serve.

Cook's tip
If you're entertaining, these are great to pass around to guests after dinner. Or, you could store them in the freezer and simply help yourself to an after-dinner treat.

(4) (4) (4) **SmartPoints value per bonbon**

Orange-cream biscuit bites

makes 24   **prep time 30 minutes**   **cook time 20 minutes**   ⊛ ⊛

Biscuit dough bases filled with a creamy cheesecake mixture and topped with raspberries. These bite-size bakes are perfectly portioned for days when you fancy something sweet.

Calorie controlled cooking spray

240g medium-fat soft cheese, softened

2 tablespoons unsalted butter

3 tablespoons skimmed milk

100g granulated sugar

90g plain flour

30g wholemeal flour

1 large egg

2 teaspoons grated orange zest, plus 1 tablespoon juice

1 teaspoon vanilla extract

24 fresh raspberries, to serve

1 teaspoon icing sugar, for dusting

1   Preheat the oven to 180°C, fan 160°C, gas mark 4. Mist a 24-hole mini muffin tin with cooking spray.

2   To make the biscuit dough, put 60g of the soft cheese and all the butter in a medium bowl, then beat with a hand-held electric whisk until smooth. Add the milk and 1 tablespoon of the granulated sugar and beat until blended. Add both flours and a pinch of salt, stirring until moist clumps form. Knead the dough in the bowl 4 times to form a ball.

3   Divide the dough into 24 pieces (about 1 heaped teaspoon each). Roll one piece of dough into a ball and use your fingers to flatten and shape into a 2.5cm round. Press into the base and sides of the prepared muffin tin. Repeat with the remaining pieces of dough.

4   To prepare the filling, put the remaining soft cheese and granulated sugar in a food processor along with the egg, orange zest and juice, and vanilla extract. Pulse until smooth and combined.

Cook's tip
Be careful not to overcook the cheesecake filling – you're looking for a bit of a wobble when you touch the top.

5   Spoon 2 teaspoons of the filling into each cup. Bake for 15-20 minutes until the filling is just set (see Cook's tip) and the pastry edges are golden. With the tip of small knife, carefully lift out each biscuit bite and let cool on a wire rack. Top each one with a raspberry, dust over the icing sugar and serve.

3 **3** **3**   SmartPoints value per biscuit bite

Coconut cinnamon rice pudding

serves 6   prep time 10 minutes   cook time 50 minutes

For a tropical twist on a British classic, add some coconut. Toasting the flakes brings a comforting, biscuity note that works brilliantly with the cinnamon.

20g coconut flakes

100g Arborio or pudding rice

1 litre skimmed milk

20g granulated sugar

½ teaspoon grated orange zest

¼ teaspoon ground cinnamon, plus extra to serve

Pinch of ground nutmeg

2 teaspoons vanilla extract

1   Preheat the oven to 160°C, fan 140°C, gas mark 4. Put the coconut flakes on a foil-lined baking sheet and bake for 4-6 minutes or until golden, then remove from the oven and set aside to cool slightly. Finely chop half the coconut flakes, reserving the rest for serving, and add to a large pan.

2   Add the rice, milk, sugar, zest, cinnamon, nutmeg and vanilla extract to the pan, and stir to combine. Bring the mixture to a gentle simmer over a very low heat, stirring so it doesn't stick to the base of the pan.

3   Simmer for 40-45 minutes, stirring occasionally at the beginning and more often as the rice swells, until the rice is tender and the consistency is creamy.

4   Divide the rice pudding between 6 small dessert dishes or glasses, scatter over the reserved toasted coconut flakes and dust with the extra cinnamon. Serve warm or chilled.

6   6   6   SmartPoints value per serving

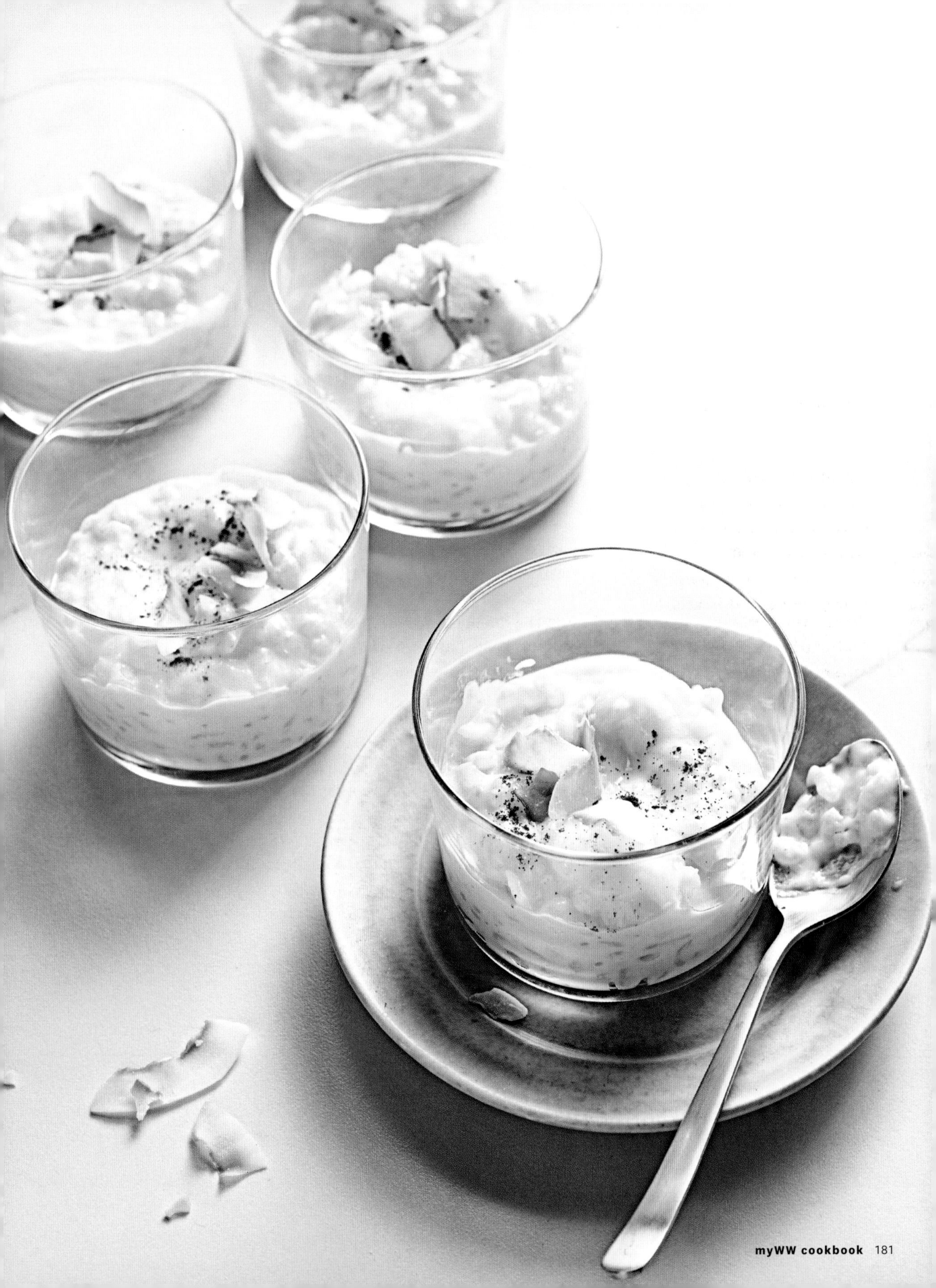

Banana choc-chip mini muffins

makes 24**freezable****prep time 15 minutes + cooling****cook time 15 minutes**

They may be tiny, but these muffins pack a lot of punch. Banana makes them naturally sweet, yogurt keeps them moist, oats bring fibre, and choc chips add a little indulgence.

Calorie controlled cooking spray

50g porridge oats

70g plain flour

70g wholemeal flour

1 teaspoon baking powder

½ teaspoon bicarbonate of soda

75ml skimmed milk

150g 0% fat natural Greek yogurt

1 egg

50g light brown soft sugar

1 ripe banana, mashed

1½ teaspoons vanilla extract

80g dark mini chocolate chips
(50% cocoa solids)

1 Preheat the oven to 190°C, fan 170°C, gas mark 5. Mist a 24-hole mini muffin tin with cooking spray.

2 Put the porridge oats, plain flour, wholemeal flour, baking powder and bicarbonate of soda into a food processor and blitz until the oats are ground as finely as the flour.

3 In a large bowl, whisk together the milk, yogurt and egg. Add the brown sugar, banana and vanilla extract. Add the flour mixture and all but 1 tablespoon of the chocolate chips to the yogurt mixture, and mix well.

4 Spoon the batter into the prepared muffin tin and scatter over the remaining chocolate chips. Bake for 15 minutes, or until a skewer inserted into the centre of a muffin comes out clean. Set aside to cool in the tin for 5 minutes, then run a knife around the inside of the holes to loosen the muffins from the tin. Turn out onto a wire rack and leave to cool completely.

The muffins can be stored in an airtight container for up to 2 days, or frozen for up to 3 months.

2 **2** **2** SmartPoints value per mini muffin

Four variations
Ice cream wafers

Fancy a sweet treat? These brilliant ideas start with plain ice cream wafers and transform them into super-simple desserts in a matter of minutes.

Strawberry cheesecake sundaes
makes 4
prep time 5 minutes

Put 20 **sugar-free ice cream wafers** (we used Tesco) in a food processor, blitz to a coarse crumb and set aside. In a medium bowl, whisk together 500g **fat-free quark**, 50g **agave syrup** and 1 teaspoon **vanilla extract** until smooth and combined. In a separate bowl, combine 300g hulled and quartered **strawberries** and the pared zest and juice of 1 **orange**. To assemble the desserts, layer the wafer crumb, quark mixture and strawberries in tall dessert or sundae glasses, then serve topped with a little extra orange zest.

5 **3** **3** SmartPoints value per serving

Choc-nut wafers
serves 4
prep time 10 minutes + cooling
cook time 5 minutes

Put 50g chopped **dark chocolate** into a microwave-safe bowl. Cook for 30 seconds on High, then stir and cook for another 30 seconds until melted. Put 12 **sugar-free ice cream wafers** (we used Tesco) on a cooling rack and drizzle over the melted chocolate. Scatter over 20g chopped **roasted hazelnuts** and set aside for 5 minutes to cool and set.

5 **5** **5** SmartPoints value per serving

Ultimate affogato
serves 2
prep time 5 minutes

Add ½ teaspoon **almond extract** to 80ml freshly brewed hot **espresso** and set aside. Working quickly, put 2 x 50ml scoops **low-calorie salted caramel ice cream** (we used Oppo) into small dessert glasses or bowls, then pour over the almond-flavoured coffee and serve immediately with 2 **sugar-free ice cream wafers** (we used Tesco) on the side of each.

3 **3** **3** SmartPoints value per serving

Blackberry & ginger Eton mess
serves 2
prep time 5 minutes + cooling
cook time 5 minutes

Roughly crush 100g halved **blackberries** and 2 teaspoons **agave syrup** together with 1 teaspoon water in a small pan. Simmer over a low heat for 2-3 minutes, or until thickened. Remove from the heat and set aside to cool completely. In a small bowl, whip 50ml **half-fat double cream alternative** using a hand-held electric whisk, until thickened. Fold in 200g **0% fat natural Greek yogurt** and a 40g grated ball **stem ginger**, followed by 3 **sugar-free ice cream wafers** (we used Tesco) broken into small pieces and the cooled compote. Spoon into dessert glasses or bowls and serve.

9 **8** **8** SmartPoints value per serving

Snacks

Four variations
Yogurt

One of the most versatile ingredients you can think of, yogurt is not just great for breakfast. Try these simple between-meal snacks you can enjoy at any time of the day.

Apricots with yogurt, honey & pistachios

serves 2
prep time 5 minutes

In a small bowl, combine 200g **fat-free natural yogurt** and 1 teaspoon **clear honey**, then set aside. Halve 3 **apricots** and remove the stones, then put them in 2 dessert bowls. Spoon over the yogurt mixture, then scatter over 15g chopped **pistachios**. Drizzle each portion with 1 teaspoon clear honey, then serve.

6 4 4 SmartPoints value per serving

Seed crumble with vanilla yogurt

Serves 1 (crumble makes 8 x 25g servings)
prep time 5 minutes
cook time 30 minutes

Preheat the oven to 160°C, fan 140°C, gas mark 2 and line a large baking tray with baking paper. Combine 100g **porridge oats**, ½ teaspoon **ground cinnamon** and 25g each of **pumpkin seeds**, **sunflower seeds** and **sesame seeds** in a mixing bowl. Put 1 **egg white** into a bowl and use a fork to whisk until frothy, then stir in 2 tablespoons **agave syrup**. Pour over the oat mixture and stir to combine. Spread the mixture over the prepared baking tray and bake for 30 minutes, stirring every 10 minutes, until the crumble is crisp and clumping together. Remove from the oven and cool on the tray, then keep in an airtight container for up to 5 days. For a single serving, mix 200g **fat-free natural yogurt** with ⅛ teaspoon **vanilla extract**, then top with 25g of the crumble.

8 4 2 SmartPoints value per serving
(25g crumble with yogurt and vanilla)

Fresh fruit with cheesecake cream

serves 1
prep time 5 minutes

In a small bowl, beat together 75g **low-fat soft cheese**, ¼ teaspoon **vanilla extract**, 1 teaspoon **lemon juice** and 2 teaspoons **agave syrup**, until combined. Stir through 75g **0% fat natural Greek yogurt** until smooth. Spoon the cheesecake cream over **fresh fruit** of your choice – we used strawberries and passion fruit.

5 4 4 SmartPoints value per serving

Herby yogurt dip

serves 4
prep time 10 minutes

In a medium bowl, combine 200g **0% fat natural Greek yogurt**, 1 large crushed **garlic clove** and the grated zest and juice of 1 **lemon**. Season to taste, then stir in 2 tablespoons each of chopped **fresh mint** and **fresh coriander**. Spoon into a serving bowl, drizzle over ½ teaspoon **extra-virgin olive oil** and serve with mixed **vegetable crudités** on the side – we used sliced cucumber and yellow peppers.

1 0 0 SmartPoints value per serving

Fruit & grain snack bars

makes 32   **prep time 15 minutes**   **cook time 15 minutes**

A portable snack that satisfies at any time of day, these little bars are full of delicious good-for-you ingredients, such as bananas, seeds, nuts and grains.

Calorie controlled cooking spray

90g dried apricots

70g dried cranberries

70g raisins

90g porridge oats

75g unsalted sunflower seeds

30g wheat bran

50g chopped pecans or walnuts

50g skimmed milk powder

30g wholemeal flour

1 teaspoon ground cinnamon

½ teaspoon salt

1 ripe banana, cut into chunks

2 eggs

100g maple syrup

1 teaspoon vanilla extract

1   Preheat the oven to 180°C, fan 160°C, gas mark 4. Mist a 22cm x 32cm baking tray with cooking spray and line with baking paper, leaving a little hanging over the edge.

2   Put the dried fruit, oats, sunflower seeds, wheat bran, nuts, milk powder, flour, cinnamon and salt into a food processor, then blitz until the dried fruit is finely chopped but not puréed. Add the banana, eggs, maple syrup, and vanilla extract and blitz again until just combined.

3   Press the fruit mixture into the prepared baking tray and bake for 15 minutes, or until golden and firm to the touch. Let cool completely in the baking tray on a wire rack, then lift out on the paper and cut into 32 bars.

The bars can be stored in an airtight container in the fridge for up to 5 days, or frozen for up to 4 months.

3 **3** **3** SmartPoints value per bar

Smoked salmon canapés

serves 1   prep time 10 minutes

A bit special and very delicious, these finger-food snacks couldn't be easier to prep. This recipe serves one, but it's easy to scale it up for sharing with friends or serving at a party.

1 slice WW Soft Malted Danish bread

1 tablespoon medium-fat soft cheese

30g smoked salmon

1 teaspoon chopped fresh dill

1 teaspoon capers

1 teaspoon finely chopped red onion

1 teaspoon grated lemon zest

1   Lightly toast the bread, then remove the crusts.

2   Spread the toast with the soft cheese and top with the salmon. Cut into 4 triangles, then scatter over the dill, capers, onion and lemon zest, and serve.

4   3   3   SmartPoints value per serving

Cook's tip
If you don't have any dill, snip over a few fresh chives instead for no extra SmartPoints.

Miso houmous

serves 8   **prep time 15 minutes**

For a change from regular houmous, try this delicious Japanese-style version that's flavoured with miso, sesame and ginger.

400g tin chickpeas in water, drained and rinsed

80g white miso paste

60ml freshly squeezed lemon juice

1 tablespoon olive oil

1 garlic clove, chopped

1 teaspoon toasted sesame oil

1 teaspoon grated fresh ginger

Small handful coriander, chopped

2 spring onions, trimmed and thinly sliced

1 teaspoon sesame seeds

Mixed vegetable crudités, for dipping (we used a mix of baby carrots, radishes and celery)

1 Put the chickpeas into a food processor along with the miso paste, lemon juice, olive oil, garlic, sesame oil and ginger. Blitz until smooth, then scrape the houmous into a serving bowl and stir in the coriander and half the spring onions.

2 Meanwhile, toast the sesame seeds in a dry frying pan for 3 minutes over a medium heat, shaking the pan occasionally, until golden.

3 Scatter the remaining spring onions and the toasted sesame seeds over the houmous and serve with the crudités.

2 **1** **1**   SmartPoints value per serving

Caesar salad cups

serves 4   prep time 15 minutes   cook time 10 minutes

Bring a touch of vibrant colour and added crunch to a buffet table spread with these Caesar salad cups – no cutlery required!

22g slice calorie controlled brown bread, cut into small cubes

½ teaspoon sunflower oil

165g cooked skinless chicken breast fillet, finely diced

2 spring onions, trimmed and finely sliced

20g Parmesan, finely grated

1 tablespoon fat-free natural yogurt

1 WW Caesar salad dressing sachet

8 Baby Gem lettuce leaves

½ punnet salad cress, snipped

1   Preheat the oven to 200°C, fan 180°C, gas mark 6. In a small bowl, toss together the bread and oil, then season and put onto a small baking tray. Bake for 5-10 minutes, until the croutons are crisp and golden.

2   In a small bowl, combine the chicken, spring onions and two-thirds of the Parmesan. In a separate bowl, whisk together the yogurt and dressing. Drizzle over the chicken mixture and toss to combine.

3   Arrange the lettuce leaves on a serving platter. Spoon the chicken mixture and croutons into the leaves, then season to taste and garnish with the cress and remaining Parmesan.

3 2 2   SmartPoints value per serving

Warm tapas-style almonds

serves 4   prep time 5 minutes   cook time 5 minutes

Make a double or triple batch of these easy-prep almonds and you'll always
have a snack ready whenever you fancy something savoury.

½ teaspoon olive oil

100g blanched whole almonds

½ teaspoon salt

¼ teaspoon paprika

Pinch cayenne pepper

1 Heat the oil in a medium, nonstick frying pan set over a
medium-high heat. Add the almonds and reduce the heat
to medium-low. Cook, shaking the pan occasionally, for
5 minutes or until the almonds are just starting to turn brown.

2 Transfer the almonds to a serving dish. Sprinkle over the salt,
paprika and cayenne pepper, then toss until evenly coated.
Serve warm.

Cook's tip
These almonds will keep
in an airtight container
for up to 1 month.

5 5 **5** **SmartPoints value per serving**

Crunchy onion rings with buttermilk dip

serves 6   prep time 20 minutes   cook time 20 minutes

These crunchy oven-baked onion rings, served with a fresh-tasting dip, are much lower in SmartPoints than the greasy, deep-fried ones you'll find in restaurants.

Calorie controlled cooking spray

60g plain flour

80g panko breadcrumbs

125ml buttermilk

1 large egg

¼ teaspoon cayenne pepper

¼ teaspoon garlic granules

3 onions, cut into 1.5cm-thick slices and then separated into rings

FOR THE BUTTERMILK DIP

120ml buttermilk

90g reduced-fat mayonnaise

1 small garlic clove, crushed

3 tablespoons chopped fresh chives

2 tablespoons chopped fresh flat-leaf parsley

½ teaspoon rice vinegar

1 Preheat the oven to 200°C, fan 180°C, gas mark 6. Mist a large nonstick baking tray with cooking spray.

2 To make the dip, whisk together all the dip ingredients in small bowl until blended, then season to taste. Set aside to allow the flavours to meld.

3 To make the onion rings, spread half the flour on a plate and all the breadcrumbs on a second plate. In a shallow bowl, whisk together the buttermilk, egg, remaining flour, cayenne pepper and garlic so you have a smooth batter, then season.

4 Coat the onion rings, five at a time, with flour. Dip them into the batter, letting any excess batter drip off, then coat with the panko breadcrumbs. Transfer to the prepared baking tray, then repeat with the remaining onions. Mist the rings with cooking spray and bake for 15-20 minutes, turning halfway through, or until the onion is tender and the coating is crisp and golden.

5 Serve the onion rings with the buttermilk dip on the side.

 **SmartPoints value per serving**

Cook's tip

Try using kefir – a cultured, fermented thick milk drink that's similar to yogurt but with a tart, sour taste – instead of buttermilk in this recipe. It brings a unique flavour, plus the added nutritional benefits of probiotics, yeast and bacteria that are good for gut health.

Blue corn nachos

serves 8   prep time 10 minutes   cook time 15 minutes

This is the perfect TV snack to share with the family.

Calorie controlled cooking spray

135g blue corn tortilla chips

400g tin pinto beans, drained and rinsed

2 plum tomatoes, chopped

2 spring onions, trimmed and sliced

1 tablespoon sliced jalapeños, drained and chopped

80g WW Reduced Fat Grated Mature Cheese

Small handful chopped fresh coriander leaves, to serve

Lime wedges, to serve

1   Preheat the oven to 200°C, fan 180°C, gas mark 6. Mist a large baking tray with cooking spray.

2   Arrange two-thirds of the tortilla chips on the prepared baking dish in a single layer. Top with the beans, tomatoes, spring onions, and jalapeños. Crush the remaining tortilla chips and scatter over the top, then scatter over the grated cheese.

3   Bake for 15 minutes, until heated through and the cheese is melted. Scatter over the coriander and serve with the lime wedges on the side.

4   3   3   SmartPoints value per serving

Cook's tip
You can find blue corn tortilla chips online and in larger supermarkets, but if you can't get hold of them, use regular corn tortilla chips instead. The SmartPoints will remain the same.

Chickpea & lemon bruschetta

makes 12   prep time 15 minutes   cook time 6-8 minutes Ⓥ ⊛ Ⓕ

Zingy fresh lemon is the star in these bruschetta bites. If you have other tinned beans on hand you can use them instead – just adjust the SmartPoints.

200g baguette, cut into 12 slices

400g tin chickpeas, drained and rinsed

¼ large red onion, finely chopped

Grated zest of 1 lemon

1 tablespoon lemon juice

2 teaspoons olive oil

1 garlic clove, crushed

Pinch cayenne pepper

¼ teaspoon paprika

Small handful fresh flat-leaf parsley, roughly chopped

1 Preheat the oven to 200°C, fan 180°C, gas mark 6. Lay the bread slices in a single layer on a large baking sheet and bake for 6-8 minutes, until golden but not completely dry all the way through. Set aside to cool.

2 Put the chickpeas into a bowl and mash using a fork, until crushed. Stir in the onion, lemon zest and juice, oil, garlic and cayenne pepper until well combined. Season to taste.

3 Spoon the chickpea mixture onto the toasts, sprinkle over the paprika and serve garnished with the parsley.

2 2 2 **SmartPoints value per bruschetta**

Banana bread

serves 12   prep time 15 minutes + cooling   cook time 50 minutes

Fresh or toasted, on its own or spread with your favourite topping – however you serve this long-lasting sesame-topped loaf, it's sure to become a new family favourite.

Calorie controlled cooking spray

125g self-raising flour

125g wholemeal flour

50g golden caster sugar

1½ teaspoons baking powder

½ teaspoon bicarbonate of soda

1 teaspoon ground cinnamon

2-3 very ripe bananas, chopped (you'll need 200g)

400g tin cannellini beans, drained, rinsed and patted dry

1½ teaspoons vanilla extract

⅛ teaspoon almond extract

50g low-fat spread, melted

1 large egg, lightly beaten

1 teaspoon sesame seeds

1 Preheat the oven to 180°C, fan 160°C, gas mark 4. Mist a 900g loaf tin with cooking spray and line with baking paper.

2 In a large mixing bowl, combine the flours, sugar, baking powder, bicarbonate of soda, cinnamon and a pinch of salt. Put the bananas, beans, vanilla and almond extracts in a food processor and blitz to a smooth purée.

3 Add the banana mixture to the dry ingredients along with the melted spread and egg. Stir to form a smooth batter, then spoon into the prepared tin. Level the surface with a spatula and scatter over the sesame seeds. Bake for 45-50 minutes, until risen and golden and a skewer inserted into the centre of the banana bread comes out clean.

4 Remove from the oven and let cool in the tin for 15 minutes, then remove from the tin to cool completely.

The loaf can be stored at room temperature in an airtight container. Serve the banana bread fresh for 2-3 days, and toasted for up to 1 week.

Cook's tip
Spread each slice of banana bread with 1 teaspoon Double berry jam (see recipe, p40). The SmartPoints will remain the same.

 **SmartPoints value per serving**

Recipe builder
Popcorn

Popcorn makes a brilliant snack just on its own, but is also a great base ingredient that you can build on with other flavours. Try these simple sweet and savoury ideas.

Basic popcorn

serves 1
prep time 1 minute
cook time 5 minutes

Mist a medium lidded pan with **calorie controlled cooking spray** and add 20g **popcorn kernels**. Cover and cook over a medium heat, shaking the pan occasionally, until the corn starts to pop. Shake constantly until all the corn has stopped popping, then remove from the heat and transfer to a bowl, discarding any unpopped corn. Serve with a sprinkling of **sea salt**.

 SmartPoints value per serving

Salted chocolate popcorn

serves 1
prep time 5 minutes
cook time 10 minutes

Preheat the oven to 180°C, fan 160°C, gas mark 4. Make a batch of **Basic popcorn** (see recipe, left), then mist the popcorn with extra **calorie controlled cooking spray** and transfer to a plastic food bag. Combine 1 teaspoon **cocoa powder**, 1 teaspoon **icing sugar** and ¼ teaspoon **sea salt** in a small bowl, then add to the bag, seal and shake well to coat. Spread the popcorn onto a baking tray and bake for 5 minutes until crisp.

 SmartPoints value per serving

Double cheese popcorn

serves 1
prep time 5 minutes
cook time 10 minutes

Preheat the oven to 200°C, fan 180°C, gas mark 6. Make a batch of **Basic popcorn** (see recipe, far left), then spread the popcorn over a baking tray and mist with extra **calorie controlled cooking spray**. Scatter over 5g finely grated **vegetarian Italian-style hard cheese**, a pinch of **English mustard powder** and a pinch of **sweet smoked paprika**. Toss to coat, then push the popcorn together into a single, tightly packed layer. Grate over 15g **half-fat mature Cheddar** and bake for 5 minutes until the popcorn is crisp, and the cheese is melted.

4 4 2 SmartPoints value per serving

Sweet & spicy popcorn

serves 1
prep time 5 minutes
cook time 10 minutes

Preheat the oven to 200°C, fan 180°C, gas mark 6. Make a batch of **Basic popcorn** (see recipe, far left), then spread the popcorn over a baking tray and drizzle over 1 teaspoon **clear honey**. Scatter over a pinch each of **cayenne pepper**, **ground cinnamon** and **sea salt**, then mist with **calorie controlled cooking spray** and toss to coat. Bake for 5 minutes until the popcorn is crisp and fragrant.

3 3 1 SmartPoints value per serving

Meal plans

Quick
& easy

A delicious, healthy meal doesn't have to be hours in the making. In 30 minutes or less, you can have any of these dishes on the table.

Monday (23) (15) (15)	**Tuesday** (23) (19) (14)
BREAKFAST	BREAKFAST
Yogurt breakfast pots p62	**Coconut, cardamom & blueberry porridge** p67
(8) (4) (4)	(5) (5) (2)
LUNCH	LUNCH
Roast chicken Waldorf salad p70	**Tuna Niçoise salad** p78
(8) (5) (5)	(5) (4) (2)
DINNER	DINNER
Griddled sea bass with lemons & tomato vinaigrette p142	**Lemony pork piccata** p128
(3) (2) (2)	(8) (8) (8)
SNACKS/DESSERT	SNACKS/DESSERT
Chickpea & lemon bruschetta p204	**Caesar salad cups** p196
(2) (2) (2)	(3) (2) (2)
Small cappuccino with skimmed milk	**150g 0% fat natural Greek yogurt topped with fresh fruit**
(2) (2) (2)	(2) (0) (0)

Wednesday (25) (21) (13)

Thursday (22) (16) (14)

Friday (24) (18) (15)

BREAKFAST
Poached eggs & bacon with hollandaise sauce p58
(7) (5) (5)

LUNCH
Overstuffed sweet potatoes p80
(9) (9) (1)

DINNER
Sage & blue cheese chicken burgers p118
(8) (7) (7)

SNACKS/DESSERT
Herby yogurt dip p188

Fresh vegetables

BREAKFAST
Green goddess fruit salad p42
(1) (1) (1)

LUNCH
Salmon, mint & cucumber baguettes p90
(8) (7) (7)

DINNER
Tex-Mex turkey steaks with sweetcorn salad p138
(6) (1) (1)

SNACKS/DESSERT
Sweet & spicy popcorn p209
(3) (3) (1)

Vegetable crudités with 2 tbsp reduced-fat houmous
(4) (4) (4)

BREAKFAST
Instant croque madame p40
(5) (3) (3)

LUNCH
Buffalo-style chicken salad p94
(5) (4) (4)

DINNER
Kimchi soba with prawns & edamame p122
(6) (4) (1)

SNACKS/DESSERT
Miso houmous p194
(2) (1) (1)

Sliced apple with 2 tbsp peanut butter
(6) (6) (6)

Veggie

Whether you're a commited vegetarian or just fancy a day or two without meat, these meal plan ideas are varied, delicious and satisfying.

Monday   **30** **23** **11**

BREAKFAST
Tex-Mex tomatoes on toast p40

LUNCH
Cheese & leek jacket potatoes p86

DINNER
Freekeh stir-fry bowls p120
9 **7** **2**

SNACKS/DESSERT
Crunchy onion rings with buttermilk dip p200

Fresh fruit
0 **0** **0**

Tuesday   **23** **19** **14**

BREAKFAST
Apple & cranberry Bircher muesli p46

LUNCH
Harissa tomato tarts p72

DINNER
Stuffed pasta shells p150
6 **6** **5**

SNACKS/DESSERT
Boiled egg

Nectarine & banana ice 'cream' p166
1 **0** **0**

| **Wednesday** (25)(21)(16) | **Thursday** (27)(22)(13) | **Friday** (27)(15)(15) |

BREAKFAST
Peanut butter, banana & agave porridge p67
(8)(7)(4)

LUNCH
Mushroom barley soup p88
(4)(4)(4)

DINNER
Smoky bean & barley burgers p158
(10)(7)(7)

SNACKS/DESSERT
Salted chocolate popcorn p208
(3)(3)(1)

Vegetable crudites with fresh salsa (no oil)
(0)(0)(0)

BREAKFAST
Avocado, lime & feta on toast p40
(8)(7)(7)

LUNCH
Courgette ribbons with mixed herb pesto & tomatoes p100
(3)(3)(3)

DINNER
Garlicky kale & bean stuffed potatoes p112
(12)(10)(1)

SNACKS/DESSERT
Banana choc-chip mini muffin p182
(2)(2)(2)

150g 0% fat natural Greek yogurt topped with fresh fruit
(2)(0)(0)

BREAKFAST
Lemon ricotta pancakes p52
(7)(7)(7)

LUNCH
Harissa, butter bean & roasted tomato soup p105
(6)(2)(2)

DINNER
Spicy corn chowder p163
(10)(5)(5)

SNACKS/DESSERT
Miso houmous p194
(2)(1)(1)

150g 0% fat natural Greek yogurt topped with fresh fruit
(2)(0)(0)

Family friendly

Only want to cook once, but still keep everyone happy? Put a smile on all their faces with these daily menus the whole family will love.

Monday   24 15 **15**

BREAKFAST
Herbed ricotta & bacon frittata p54
7 4 **4**

LUNCH
Roasted tomato soup p104
2 2 **2**

DINNER
Kiev-style chicken with garden greens salad p108
9 6 **6**

SNACKS/DESSERT
Blue corn nachos p202
4 3 **3**

150g 0% fat natural Greek yogurt topped with fresh fruit
2 0 **0**

Tuesday   29 21 **12**

BREAKFAST
Yogurt breakfast pots p62
8 4 **4**

LUNCH
Cheese & leek jacket potatoes p86
12 9 **2**

DINNER
Sweet potato lasagne with turkey & sage p130
5 4 **2**

SNACKS/DESSERT
Banana bread p206
4 4 **4**

Vegetable crudités with fresh salsa (no oil)
0 0 **0**

| Wednesday | 22 17 15 | Thursday | 30 19 16 | Friday | 22 17 16 |

BREAKFAST
**Green goddess
fruit salad** p42
1 1 1

LUNCH
**Chicken parmigiana
open sandwiches** p102
9 8 8

DINNER
**Bangers, baked beans
& butternut squash
bake** p154
6 4 4

SNACKS/DESSERT
**Double cheese
popcorn** p209
4 4 2

**150g 0% fat natural
Greek yogurt topped
with fresh fruit**

2 0 0

BREAKFAST
**Veggie omelette
muffins** p48
8 5 5

LUNCH
**Salmon, white bean
& pasta salad** p96
7 5 2

DINNER
**Beef & pinto
bean chilli** p134

10 6 6

SNACKS/DESSERT
**Vegetable crudités
with fresh salsa (no oil)**
0 0 0

**Strawberry
cheesecake
sundaes** p184

5 3 3

BREAKFAST
**Eat-your-greens
yogurt muffins** p50
6 5 5

LUNCH
**Mexican-style
chicken soup** p98
6 3 3

DINNER
**Stuffed pasta
shells** p150
6 6 5

SNACKS/DESSERT
**Herby yogurt dip with
vegetable crudités** p188
1 0 0

**Fruit & grain
snack bars** p190
3 3 3

Recipe index

Recipe index

SmartPoints index

Green

SmartPoints index

Purple

WW PUBLISHING TEAM

Samantha Rees, Harriet Joy, Jessica O'Shea, Nicola Kirk. With thanks to Shelley Fletcher.

FOR SEVEN PUBLISHING LTD

FOOD

Food editor: Sarah Cook

Recipes: Sarah Cook, Anita Janusic, Ella Tarn, Terry Grieco Kenny, Frank Melodia, Angela Nilsen, Carol Prager

EDITORIAL

Editor-in-chief: Helen Renshaw

Editor: Christine Faughlin

Sub-editors: Ward Hellewell, Sasha Turnbull

DESIGN & PHOTOGRAPHY

Art director: Liz Baird

Photographer: Ant Duncan

Additional photography: Ian Harrison, David Malosh

Food stylists: Sarah Cook, Simon Andrews

Prop stylists: Davina Perkins, Suzie Myers

ACCOUNT MANAGEMENT

Senior account manager: Gina Cavaciuti

Group publishing director: Kirsten Price

PRODUCTION

Print lead: Liz Knipe

Colour reproduction by F1 Colour

Printed in Italy by Rotolito S.p.A

Seven ^{C3}

Produced by Seven Publishing Ltd on behalf of WW International, Inc. Published December 2019. All rights reserved. No part of this publication may be reproduced, stored in retrieval system or transmitted in any form by any means, electronic, mechanical photocopying, recording or otherwise, without the prior written permission of Seven Publishing Ltd. First published in Great Britain by Seven Publishing Ltd.

Seven Publishing Ltd,
3-7 Herbal Hill, London EC1R 5EJ
www.seven.co.uk

This book is copyright under the Berne Convention. No reproduction without permission.

All rights reserved.
10 9 8 7 6 5 4 3 2 1

©2020 WW International, Inc. Nothing may be reprinted in whole or in part without permission from the publisher. Editorial and art produced by Seven Publishing Ltd. The WW Coin Logo, SmartPoints, ZeroPoint, and myWW are the trademarks of WW International, Inc.

A CIP catalogue record for this book is available from the British Library.

ISBN: 978-1-9996673-7-5